HOW TO ANALYZE PEOPLE & BODY LANGUAGE MASTERY 2 IN 1

A PRACTICAL GUIDE TO SPEED READING PEOPLE, INCREASING EMOTIONAL INTELLIGENCE (EQ) & PROTECTING AGAINST MANIPULATION BY DARK PSYCHOLOGY

WESTLEY ARMSTRONG

DEVON HOUSE
PRESS

CONTENTS

INTRODUCTION

How many times has someone told you something but meant a different thing altogether? Words are easy to say, I can tell you anything I want. But how do you know if I'm being honest? How do you know if I have an ulterior motive, maybe even a bad one? How can you tell when a politician is trying to deceive you? How can you tell a conman from an honest merchant?

You can just read it! "Hold on," you may say, "we read words, and you just told me that words can be manipulated..." Yes, words can – actually very often *are* – manipulated! But we don't just read words! We also read smiles, lips, hands, even feet... I don't mean like palm reading though... What I mean is analyzing body language and that huge set of nonverbal signals we produce all the time!

Did you know that most of what we "say" is nonverbal? Technically we should say "communicate", but the point is that 60% of what we communicate on average is nonverbal. Only 40% of communication is made up of words (written, spoken, sung...)

So, don't you think it's strange that in all our communication studies (from learning to speak to learning English to studying journalism and reading Shakespeare) basically all we learn is how to read words?

No wonder there are so many misunderstandings. *We only learn to make sense of 40% of all we communicate!* Now, imagine if you could understand 60, 70 or even 80% of what people are actually telling you!

And before we go further, let's pause a second... You may be thinking, "Yes, but reading body language and nonverbal signals is a lot of work..." I fully understand you. Verbal language can already be tricky with some people. Just imagine politicians or insurance agents... They twist words, they use strange terms, they play with ambiguity... Fine but...

...Reading nonverbal communication does not need to be a hassle nor a hard task. You will not be taking out a notebook and jotting down all signs all the time... Like all things you learn, if you "digest it" well, it will become second nature to you. It will become spontaneous, effortless, automatic... Like driving a car in fact...

It is mainly a matter of becoming conscious of what's "beyond words and encoded in gesturers" and equipping yourself with a good set of "reading tools". Then it's all downhill!

And in fact, people who are good at reading body language do it all the time and naturally, almost unconsciously. Statistically, women are better than men at this. But there is more... Everybody does it to some extent, but we are not always very conscious of it...

Think about it... Do you remember any time when someone told you something, but you just didn't believe it, because "something wasn't just right?" Maybe that saved you a few bucks or even from worse, like a bad relationship? But you still can't put your finger on "that thing that did not click..." That's because it wasn't a word, nor a sentence... It was a nonverbal sign that you read without being aware of it!

And I will let you in on a secret... I too was very bad at reading nonverbal language. And in fact, as a child I was frustrated. People took advantage of me regularly and, well, I faced big disappointments. But then, when I studied psychology at university, I realized that most of what happens in our mind is not conscious, let alone verbal! I realized that if something is irrational, it cannot be verbal. Words express rational thoughts... But how about all creative, emotional and simply non rational thinking?

Then I studied pedagogy, and I learned that a good teacher is not one who says the right words... But someone who conveys concepts through many means of communication. And that only a minority of students have a primarily verbal way of learning. Some have visual learning natures, other kinesthetic (based on movement) etc.

Funny, isn't it? Verbal communication isn't even the most common natural learning method, but I trust your experience of school is one of – how to describe it – lots of words and verbosity?

So, I changed my course of study after my degree. I was a very rational person, I realized. But I wanted to learn all about "the other side of human intelligence and behavior". And I spent years researching it...

The consequences? Well, to start with, when I was all rational, I was easy prey to deceit and grifters... *After learning to analyze nonverbal communication, it became much harder to deceive me.* Now, think about it, I am not! So, if you are like I was, the one dishonest people can "smell at a distance" or even if you just get conned every now and then... You too will avoid a lot of problems.

And don't take my words as read (sorry about the pun)! It's not just me saying that analyzing nonverbal communication has massive positive effects on your life. It's science! There are loads of studies I could refer you to, but a recent one on how, for example, this can change your family relations is 'The Nonverbal Communication of Positive Emotions: An Emotion Family Approach' by psychologist Disa A. Sauter from Amsterdam University, which appeared in the peer reviewed psychology journal *Emotion Review* in July 2017. It concludes that most positive emotions are communicated only non-verbally! Think about how much happiness we are missing out on...

But *the benefits will heap up for you as they did for me* if you learn to analyze nonverbal communication... There are so many that I would not know where to start...

Your social relationships will improve a lot! This includes your relationships with significant others (friends, family, partner etc.) but also with people you are "just acquainted with" or you make casual encounters with.

And yes, *also with your colleagues at school or at work...* And this can make *a huge difference in your quality of life...* Think about it, what do you do as soon as you get home? Most people complain about this or that colleague, school friend, teacher, or, most frequently – boss! They can make our life a misery. And if you can bypass their verbal communication, you will be the one in charge now.

Do you want some more? *Your professional life will improve a lot!* You will actually see it change before your eyes. Again, if you only understand verbal signals at work, you miss out on a whole sphere of communication and information you could use for your actual work and tasks, for your colleagues and (why not?) for your career.

You will grow in people's esteem. Yes, because every time we miss a clue, every time we misunderstand a point (even hidden ones), we actually make fools of ourselves. Yes, our friends and family are understanding... but it's the cumulative effect that matters... And don't forget – people remember these small events subconsciously.

You'll become more intelligent. Especially, you'll become *more emotionally intelligent.* You may've heard of this, because it is a very important topic in psychology and self-development these days. Emotional intelligence is very much based on nonverbal communication. *People with good emotional intelligence are on average happier and more successful than those who are lacking.*

As a consequence, *your quality of life will skyrocket. You'll be happier, more confident, you'll waste much less time solving problems you didn't foresee,* and you'll have better relationships.

Last, but by no means least, *you'll not be manipulated easily.* Let's call a spade a spade... When you watch an ad, you're exposed to a picture or short clip made by an expert in manipulation and with a lot of means at his or her disposal... We're being manipulated all the time.

Every time you buy something and after a while you say, "Why in the world did I buy it?" the answer is always the same: you have been manipulated into doing it! *Politicians are professional manipulators.* This is nothing new. They have been so since the times of Classical Greece! Their speeches were masterpieces of crowd manipulation... Now they just got better and have bigger means.

But hold on – do you know that politicians (like actors and actresses) are literally trained to use body language and nonverbal communication? It's one of the most important parts of their training and success! "He looks presidential," we say, because he (one day she) learnt to stand, look, move, use his hands etc. in a way that projects confidence and calm.

You're right! Politicians and professional con-people are a step ahead. But let me tell you a secret: even for them it's very hard, actually impossible to hide their real thoughts. A little twist in Bill Clinton's lip cast deep doubts about his "straight face" and defense in the Monica Lewinsky case...

And you must have seen psychologists analyze people's nonverbal communication on TV. You can do it too now. And if politicians and grifters have an advantage now, it is one more reason to start soon!

Taking about that... Do you know when the next manipulator, conman or dishonest colleague will metaphorically knock on your life's door? No, but it may well be tomorrow!

Do you realize how every day you spend without being capable of analyzing people's body language and other signs is a day you miss out on a lot of happiness and confidence?

How long are you ready to wait before you do something to improve those relationships that frustrate you so much? And even good relationships have frustrating moments, we all know!

Now, honestly think about it: *you could be on the way to solving all these problems in minutes...* Or you could put it off, and waste valuable time.

And *this book is really based on actual research; it is scientific in everything it says.*

But *this book is also a nice read!* True, there is hard science behind all the *strategies, skills and even exercises* in this book. But you may have guessed that we want to make this experience pleasurable, even bubbly. I told you I studied pedagogy at postgrad level (the science of teaching and learning). And you know rule number one of learning? Statistically *people learn better when they are having fun!* There goes another stuffy urban myth out of the window... lessons didn't need to be boring at school...

And *this book is also practical.* In the end, you need to learn *to analyze people's nonverbal language – not about it!* There are activities and exercises you can carry out without disturbing your daily life. They are short, but also "noninvasive". Let me explain... They are designed so that you can do them while you go about your daily life... When you are shopping, when you are on the bus etc. I don't want to take more of your time than is necessary.

You will see real and visible changes in your life. The promotion at work won't be immediate maybe, but you'll see improved relationships, confidence and in the overall quality of your life.

It's sad that analyzing nonverbal communication is not taught at school! *Think how many lives it would improve...* But hey, we should not cry over spilled milk, instead we should try to do something about our gaps...

And now you know what to do, and you know it is only a click away, I wish you a good read?

FUNDAMENTALS OF BODY LANGUAGE

WHY BODY LANGUAGE?

I f you still need convincing about the importance of body language, let me show you a quotation by writer, trainer and consultant Allen Ruddock:

"Your body communicates as well as your mouth. Don't contradict yourself."

— ALLEN RUDDOCK

There are two points we can get from this statement:

1. That if you understand body language, you also understand when people's words don't match their nonverbal communication.
2. That if you understand body language, you can improve your nonverbal communication and become more convincing, confident, trusted, and even respected.

It's a win-win situation. If you're aware of other people's body language you become more aware of your own as well. It's logical, isn't it?

But let me ask you a question. Do you think it is easier to be aware of:

1. Your own body language?
or
2. Other people's body language?

Decided? Now, here's the truth. It's far easier to be aware of other people's. And this is primarily what we are concerned about. But you will also see improvements in yours. It's not fully automatic. Meaning that you'll not automatically apply all you have learned about other people to yourself. We all know that the most difficult person to observe is oneself.

But you *will become more aware of your own body language,* which is necessary to then correct it.

Now, why understand body language? Do you know what they say about job interviews? That the panel decide if you get the job or not in the first 60 or even 30 seconds? "Nice waste of time," you may think… I agree. But let's say that not everything gets decided in the first minute or so…

It is more likely that they decide if you make the (final) cut in those few seconds… But what interests us is this: how many words do you actually say in the first 30 seconds?

The answer is very few, and none of them of any relevance at all to the job. It's usually like this:

Panel: "Good morning."

You: "Good morning."

Panel: "Did you find the place alright?"

You: "Oh yes!"

End of the 30 seconds...

So, their decision about your whole future cannot be based on these words, can it? In fact, it is based on the huge set of *nonverbal signals we give away when we meet someone.*

We will see that there are times when nonverbal communication goes into over-drive. And one of these moments is when you meet new people or start an inter-action in any case. While they decide if the way you stand, walk, shake hands, even dress or look around the room give them the "right impression" for you to be a valid candidate... well, you can do the same to them!

You can see if they actually like you, if they trust you, if they are interested or they are thinking about the next candidate... *They will not tell you; but they will show you.*

We briefly talked about it in the introduction, but here are some key reasons why *body language shapes and even determines our quality of life!*

Body language is key to social relationships

Think about that school mate no one ever cared about... That wallflower... Look at her or his body language? Do you want to bet that she or he had most of these in varying degrees?

- Slouching shoulders
- Often lowered his or her gaze
- Shabby or uninteresting clothes (accessories, shoes, hairstyle etc.)
- Hunching posture
- Often crossed his or her arms
- Feet pointing inward (ok, you may not have noticed it)

Basically your "missed friend's body language" told people to stay away. No wonder they did it... And this is not necessarily because that person (you now feel sorry for, I know!) actually wanted it. Our minds are more complex than that... Maybe that was all due to a lack of confidence... Maybe it simply meant, "Stay away unless you are the most trustworthy and non-judgmental person in the world"?

Yes, in most cases that body language means just that... But we don't know it. Especially as teenagers... How many people have met horrible teens because we couldn't read their actual signals to us? Here is a super reason to learn body language in my view...

And if you were one of those, then you really know what I mean...

Body language affects your success (at work but not just)

There's more to life than work. There are family relations, friends, hobbies etc. And body language does affect how successful you are at all these. Here, both analyzing body language and using positive body language can make a huge difference to your life.

We know it implicitly, don't we, that "successful people *look successful.*" Now, remember the wallflower in your class? How many successful people slouch? And I am a sloucher by nature, so I say it out of personal experience.

Allow me a personal tip from my heart, in fact... If you do slouch, by all means correct it. Please, please, please do! Your life will change like you wouldn't even dream!

And this leads us to the next point...

Body language makes you "safe or vulnerable"

Talking about slouching and the way you walk. Do you know that people who walk with their shoulders out are far less likely to be mugged or assaulted (in a dark alley?) So, *body language can even improve your very physical safety!*

You see how even criminals act upon body language... And I am sure you know about it. They look around for someone who "looks vulnerable" and that's how (consciously or unconsciously) they choose their victims.

Yet again – and vice versa! You too can spot someone with bad intentions from their body language. Follow me... We often "assess people's intentions" using the wrong tools. Very often they are prejudices the media and society force on us like:

- People with an unkempt look
- People who look "different" one way or another
- Young and tall males
- People with tattoos
- People with scars
- Unfortunately, even people with a darker skin than ours.

This leads only to the perpetuation of stereotypes and prejudice. How about if you knew how to tell if someone actually *does have negative and aggressive intentions* independently from these prejudices?

Let's look at nature for a lesson. Have you ever seen a lion walk bang in the middle of a herd of zebras and they just don't care? Of course, you have. So, zebras don't have a prejudice against lions. But as soon as the lion gets hungry, his attitude and body language change and the zebras start running!

You see, even nature uses body language as a tool of survival... And we still don't... Instead, *well trained officials (like FBI and CIA agents) are literally taught to spot body language signs that show a hidden threat.*

There's no reason why you should not know them too!

Body language makes you less "gullible"

Let's play this game... Joe and Sarah go to the market to buy groceries... Joe is really careful, he has his eyes fixed on the apples, potatoes, zucchini and tomatoes he is buying... Sarah, on the other hand, when she is buying something, she does not look at it... No... she looks around and in particular, she looks up, at the merchant or seller.

Who will end up with the best deals? The chances are that while Joe is staring at his tomatoes, the dishonest merchant feels perfectly safe! Yes, that's the word. Safe. The best way to fend off someone's grift is to look at them straight in the eyes. So, Joe may be thinking that the apples look fine while the dishonest merchant is fixing the scales...

Try it even as a game. Call a friend and try to play a little trick on her or him... For example, offer them a glass of wine (or a coffee) and then try to take it away... But looking at her/him straight in the eyes... Can you feel how difficult it is? You will literally feel frozen, or as if there's a huge energy in your body that you need to overcome...

Now look away and you already feel you only need to say something along the lines of, "Hey there's a squirrel!" and the trick is done!

Looking at the body language of the person you are striking a deal with is the best way to get a good deal (or dropping the deal if you don't trust him/her).

Body language is fun!

Allow me a personal touch as the last reason why learning nonverbal communication is good. It is actually fun to read how people move, stand, smile, their little strange gestures... It really fills your day with beautiful details. In my view, it makes you love the human psychology and behavior even more...

And it turns you into a good writer, if you have literary ambitions... Just think about what great writers have in common, an attention to detail about body language... *Body language is the best way to present a character...*

Aw, I was forgetting: Agatha Christie's Poirot! Of course, great detectives are also great body language readers!

HISTORY OF BODY LANGUAGE

Let's play another game, shall we? Okay, I'll give you some well-known names and you need to tell me what these people have in common. Newton, Darwin, Einstein, Marie Curie, Freud, Galileo, Mendel... Of course, they all had a great role in the history of science...

Like all sciences, even body language has a history. Many people will argue that it started in the Seventeenth Century, but I am a maverick and I will argue that, in some ways, we can push it well before that. Maybe not as a *"conscious and rational study of how people communicate non-verbally"* but as the *"awareness and symbolic representation of how people communicate non-verbally".* In the end we do not start the history of physics with Newton (we go back to at least Zeno, an early Greek philosopher!)

Anyway, my point in telling you this is that civilizations have been culturally aware of body language, even if they looked at it from a less scientific perspective than today. So, how far can we go? Look at a hieroglyph, that far back, yes! Do you notice that the way the body is positioned has a symbolic and expressive meaning? I know, they don't tell you at school, but in Egyptian art, you give with the left hand and receive with the right hand. A habit still strong in many cultures around the world.

This was not just a "ritual" though. The left hand is connected with the right side of the brain, the less rational and more emotional side of the brain. Giving with the left means giving "with the heart". It's a sign of honesty.

Fact is, the Egyptians left us a large set of "standardized gestures", even ritualized ones, but no actual textbook of analysis. So, in their case, we cannot talk about a conscious analysis of body language (not that we know of).

But this keeps going through art till the modern times. You will see in most paintings the importance of people is represented by *proxemics.* This is where people stand in relation to one another, and it is one of the things we use to analyze nonverbal communication.

So, kings stand higher up than their subjects in almost every painting. Protagonists go in the middle, standing and sitting down are not casual etc. But again, this is not scientific analysis; it only shows that the awareness of body language has never wavered over the centuries – actually millennia.

It is true though that we started looking at body language in a rational, empirical and overall scientific way at the beginning of the Seventeenth Century. Of course, that was a time when science was starting to assert its method. In 1605, famous English philosopher (civil servant, secret agent etc.) Francis Bacon, published a book *The Advancement of Learning* (the whole title is *Of the Proficience and Advancement of Learning, Divine and Human*) and in it he is alleged to be the first who actually linked the meaning of words with that of gestures, with a famous statement:

"As the tongue speaketh to the ear, so the gesture speaketh to the eye."

— FRANCIS BACON

Like all scientific fields, body language analysis needs a *starting hypothesis* (like "the world is round") and this then needs to find evidence in real data. Those were the beginning of this new science, and that was the starting point.

For us, Bacon's statement may sound totally granted and commonsense. But every idea needs to be checked and then proved or disproved with facts and data in science, even the most obvious. And in fact, it took decades before someone actually took Sir Francis Bacon's statement seriously enough to check his theory with data.

It was the year 1644 and an English doctor (physician) and philosopher now forgotten actually looked at one single part of our body, our hand, and set out to describe all its gestures and their meaning. His name was John Bulwer and the book had the strange title, *Chrinologia, or the Naturall Language of the Hand* ("natural" with a double L; that was the "fancy spelling" of the time).

In science, we often start with a long list of correspondences and patterns. So, Carl Linnaeus is a founding father of biology, because he spent years categorizing plants and animals (he invented the double Latin name we still use nowadays).

In the title of Bulwer's book, however, there is more than just a list confirming that a certain gesture corresponds to a certain meaning, which proved Bacon's statement... There is the idea that all hand gestures are natural...

This is important for different reasons:

1. It states that hand gestures are not a social and cultural product, but they are fully spontaneous.
2. It states that hand gestures always have the same meaning.

Both statements, we will find out later, are not fully correct. We now know that *some gestures are cultural products* (and Italians prove it all the time!) But at the time, science was in the grip of a century (millennia) long debate: *nature vs nurture.* This debate continues nowadays (is intelligence genetic or cultural, how about the "cancer gene"? or is it only pollution and the environment that causes it?).

Nowadays science tends to take a middle position in this debate: there are some natural (genetic etc.) factors as well as environmental (culture, pollution etc.) factors.

This debate is so core to science and long that we still have two schools... And along the line, even towering figures of science took part in the debate, and one in particular Charles Darwin, used body language even as evidence for his famous Theory of Evolution.

It was the year 1872, 13 years after Darwin published his controversial *On the Origin of Species* (full title *On the Origin of Species by Means of Natural Selection, or Preservation of Favoured Races in the Struggle for Life...* you couldn't fit the average book title into a tweet back then!) Anyway... You must have seen those paintings of chimpanzee faces that express emotions like human beings. This picture became famous and even a worldwide scandal!

Why? Put simply, Darwin wrote a book, *The Expression of Emotions in Man and Animals* where he used facial expressions to show the similarities between humans and animals. The closer we were on his evolutionary tree, the more similar the facial expressions were. And this was used as evidence for his famous theory.

As a note, this is the book that makes us believe that Darwin said that "humans come from apes", while he actually never said that, and he refused to say it all his life. So, body language analysis finally got into the spotlight of science, with a book that shook the academic world the same way as 'Like a Virgin' shook popular culture in the 80s.

You see that Darwin took Bulwer's position? He followed his lead and said that "because humans and naturally related animals express themselves with similar facial expressions", it must mean that "facial expressions are produced naturally and not culturally". This is what he said for us, for psychologists and those who study body language.

In reality he said the opposite for biology: "because facial expressions are produced naturally" then the fact that they are similar between humans and other species means that "humans and other species are closely related". From a philosophy of science point of view this is a circular argument. You prove a theory with another unproven theory.

In fact, nowadays we know that not all gestures are congenital, or of natural origin. In Bulgaria, they nod sideways to say "yes" and up and down to say "no" ... The rest of the world does the opposite... There is nothing in the DNA that makes it so, therefore it must be a cultural gesture.

But science is not fixed in time, and things improved from the point of view of body language... While Darwin was talking about apes and humans, another towering figure in the history of science, philosophy and above all psychology came along: Dr Sigmund Freud. His impact on psychology and psychoanalysis is colossal but he also gave us one concept that we sorely needed to understand body language:

"The mind is like an iceberg; it floats with about one seventh of its bulk above water."

— (SIGMUND FREUD, *THE UNCONSCIOUS,* 1915)

Nice metaphor, but what does it mean for us? It means that the main source of our behavior is not our conscious will and mind, but our unconscious! This is huge in terms of body language.

Freud allows us to move away from the rather academic debate of nature vs. nurture to new frontiers when it comes to body language analysis. You see, now that we know that most of our gestures, facial expressions etc. are not "meant", not "planned" and not even conscious, we can use these gestures and expressions to look behind the façade that people put on when talking.

We can analyze body language to look beyond what people want us to believe and "read" what they actually mean. Body language analysis becomes then the main tool people have to understand what people actually feel, think, want etc. Basically, now we can tell a fake smile from a real smile, at the simplest level...

Luck strikes again, and it's star studded! When Hollywood was enchanting millions with its popular movies, actors and actresses had to learn to speak, but without audio! The first films were silent in fact, and they had to improve their facial expressions and body language to communicate to their audience.

They borrowed heavily on the long tradition of the theatre, and you can see that the facial expressions and movements of early movie stars are somewhat exaggerated and stylized... But it gave drama teachers a huge chance to study actual face expressions and natural gestures, a databank of human behavior that still forms the bedrock of modern studies.

Those were the early years of the Twentieth Century, but then two horrifying wars came along and science was busy with the "war effort". But as the Second World War came to a close, the world found itself with an amazing new face...

It was the face of the 1950s, that decade we can describe with those pastel ads of washing machines and vacuum cleaners... And those adverts are full of body language analysis... The housewife who "smiles to the camera", the husband coming back from work and picking up his children for a hug – unrealistically smiling, of course!

And while companies employed professionals who told us with gestures and facial expressions why we would be happier with a washing machine rather than the new cake mix, a US anthropologist by the name of Ray Birdwhitshell was funding *kinesics*, the science of reading "facial expression, gestures, posture and gait, and visible arm and body language."

He's basically the father of body language analysis. By now, we had all we needed for a full-blown scientific field:

- A *sound theory* on which to build the field.
- A *large body of data* to study.

What really matters from now on is actually the growing body of evidence collected and the precision of analysis that professionals all over the world have been learning and displaying.

Body language can be used in court as well as for psychoanalysis. It has become a reliable way of understanding what goes on "behind the scenes" when politicians or other famous people are under scrutiny...

In the meantime, however, the long argument between nature and nurture has continued. So, zoologist Desmond Morris published *The Naked Ape* in 1967 where he stated that humans resort to animalistic behavior when under pressure. He looked at the behavior of people in cities to do so. This of course wanted to prove the fact that body language is fully natural.

Unfortunately, "animalistic" is a very personal definition, in itself a cultural one... But those were times when science leaned towards the "all is genetically motivated" theory, and even our field felt that shift.

And it was in the 1970s that US psychologists Paul Ekman and Wallace Friesen produced a long, articulated and consistent body of work that resulted in *FACS*, or *Facial Action Coding System.* This is very important because it gives us a sort of "dictionary of facial expressions", including clear ways of detecting deception. You can understand how useful this has been for investigators all over the world.

But it is also important that they looked at the cross-cultural patterns and similarities of these expressions. They are not the same in all people from all over the world. And the similarities are stronger where cultural identities are more similar. They came out with a synthesis of the nature vs. nurture debate. According to them, there are universal signs (a universal non-verbal code) but also cultural codes that "mask it", cover it or changes it.

So, coming to the present time, where are we now? We are in a very good place with body language analysis... *We have a large body of data to analyze all nonverbal communication,* from facial expressions to proxemics and much more.

We also know that *the analytical methods we use do work.* We are sure about it because it has been tested over and over again for decades, and the results are reliable.

And what's happened to the nature vs nurture leitmotif of the history of body language studies? Let's say that scholars are getting on "fairly well". They still argue, and that seems to be their nature (a pun, again...) but they argue less.

Basically, there are two *models* that scholars use to describe the different theories:

- *The cultural equivalence model,* which believes that the *main cause of body language is natural...*
- *The cultural advantage model,* which states that culturally similar people understand each other's nonverbal language better. So, *culture is key to body language.*

In 2008, Jessica Tracy and Richard Robins published an interesting study entitled 'The Nonverbal Expression of Pride: Evidence for cross cultural recognition' (*Journal of Personality and Psychology*). In it, they allege that pride and shame have the same overall body language all over the world. This is important because we may be starting to find archetypes of body language, and in science and especially psychology, discovering a set of archetypes is a huge step full of opportunities for future developments.

BE WARNED!

You know now that body language analysis is a serious science, with a long history and some very, very famous contributors like Freud and Darwin. Like mathematics or physics, or psychology itself though, it is a double-edged sword! So... Be warned!

Be warned because *when you have a powerful tool at your disposal, like body language analysis, you have responsibilities.*

It's like when you are a journalist, a politician, or a social service agent... You have the power to change people's lives. Well, I would say that more than the "bare power" (what a disgusting concept) we should look at it like this: *you have the responsibility of using it in the respect of others if not for their own good.*

Imagine a doctor who uses her or his knowledge to hurt patients! They can, of course, but they literally swear an oath not to do it. Psychologists too have a professional code. It states that you will *never use your knowledge or skills to harm anyone.* And you are going to learn some of this knowledge and skills... So, *use them wisely but above all responsibly.*

Be warned because *you can make mistakes.* And I don't mean only at the first stages. Even great experts at their fields make mistakes. Napoleon lost at Waterloo, and yet he was the greatest general on Planet Earth. Einstein made famous mistakes as a scientist. But Einstein was an honest man and he admitted them.

But when your mistake has already caused some consequences, admitting it is useless. Imagine you misinterpret a friend's body language and you abandon that friendship. Years later you find out you were wrong. Fine, you can admit it as much as you want, but that's not going to give you back your friend! You could try to make up, and that would need some talking and convincing. But what are the chances of you two actually having as good a friendship as before? And even then, the lost years would be lost forever, you can't turn back time. How about if your friend passes away before you make up?

Be warned, *because you are dealing with people's lives, including your own.*

Let's play a "specular game". This is quite common in psychology. I'll show you. Imagine that your boss has not really favored you at work because s/he misunderstands your personality. This is actually very common and if it is not happening to you now, it may have happened in the past and will very likely happen in the future...

You very likely (did/will) miss out on opportunities because of this "personality reading" mistake. And that means giving up on that holiday of your dreams... It's not a little thing... Or seeing others make careers steps while you stay behind... frustration follows... in the long run, this is a major cause of depression...

Now, let's turn the mirror... You are that boss. And we all are "bosses" in some areas of our lives. I am the boss in the kitchen at home, for example. Do you realize the impact you could have on other people's lives, even those close to you? Your family, your friends?

Be warned, *because analyzing body language should not go to your head.* You should always keep a humble and modest approach to your knowledge. Knowing more than other people does not make you better than them nor does it give you any rights over them.

Be warned, *because there is always more you can learn.* You will get to an excellent level with this book, I promised it and it will happen. But remember that there are people who have more experience than you, even than me – actually. It's a bit like with everything, with history... You know a lot, but someone will know more than you... So, in case you are in doubt, consult more experienced people about it.

Psychologists, psychotherapists, psychoanalysts etc. are usually very good at reading body language. Don't be afraid to ask a friend from those professions if you are not sure about an analysis. There are other people too, of course who can help you. And this leads me to my next point.

Be warned, *a hurried analysis is never a good analysis. Always leave the door of doubt open.* An analysis may be good, convincing, even crushingly convincing, but there is always the chance that you missed something. A good professional always keeps the "I made a mistake" option open. Not the other way around. People who are sure about everything they do are not professionals, they are bullies and very likely with personal issues...

Be warned, *because there are cultural differences.* From our brief history of body language analysis, you know that the idea that we all have the same body language all over the world has been abandoned. In Arabic countries, for example, you do not point with your hands; that is rude. Imagine one of them reading our body language and not taking the cultural "language" into account...

Be warned, *because you cannot see everything.* You will mainly see people from one point of view, at a particular moment and in a place. Sometimes there are parts of the body you cannot see, and that may change your analysis if you saw them.

But also, the time matters. Maybe someone looks fidgety and nervous and you interpret it as dishonesty? Fair guess from what you know. But how about if I told you that this person is waiting for an important health test result? Or a telephone call from his or her partner after a massive row? Or that s/he is about to simply miss the bus home and you are holding him or her behind?

We will look at how *the context is part and parcel of the analysis.* But keep in mind that you will never know "all the context", that is humanely impossible, so, think accordingly.

What does it mean in practice? *Does it mean you should avoid analyzing body language?*

I would not think so. You need to train; you need to learn. It means, however that:

- *You should not act on your analysis unless you have to, and you are sure about it.* If you suspect that someone is about to grift you and you wish to cut the conversation, by all means do! But before you take away an opportunity from someone (a job, for example) on the basis of your analysis, think twice.

- *You should be particularly careful when emotions and other people's lives are concerned.* If your analysis just tells you that you will not buy that particular phone because the merchant was not honest, you have all my sympathy. If you want to change a relationship based on your analysis, I must call for caution.
- *Distinguish between analyzing body language and acting upon it.* The beauty of school is that you get to learn about the world without the consequences... You learn about a war without acting upon it... The same should be with learning about body language, learn how to read it, practice it etc. But then do not act upon it especially when it involves relationships. Do it only when you are near 100% sure.

On a sad note, talking about school... the only area where we are not protected by simulation (we learn about history without actually starting one, about gravity without crashing a plane etc....) is in social relationships... We learn about friends and love by actually living real relationships... There is no simulation there!

But this last point remains as a final thought... From the point of view of a psychologist, knowing about the human mind, society, how to analyze people etc. is beautiful... But *nothing compares with the beauty and sacredness itself of human feelings, thoughts, experience and of course relationships.*

Be professional and put these values first.

2

THE SCIENCE BEHIND BODY LANGUAGE

W ho studies body language? I mean, which field does it belong to? By now, you should know that body language analysis is not a "random practice" with no scientific value. As we said, it is even used by investigators, intelligence agents, etc. Basically, *there is hard science behind body language analysis.*

In the previous chapter we looked briefly at the history of this science. But you may be a bit confused because there are psychologists, biologists (actually Darwin was a theologian!), anthropologists etc. So, where does body language analysis fall?

Like most scientific developments, *it draws on many fields and disciplines, but as a whole, it falls roughly within psychology.*

The main fields it is related to are:

- Psychology
- Sociology
- Anthropology
- Linguistics
- Semiotics

- Biology
- Neurology

But we should not forget the contributions of the arts, like drama, painting, and the cinema... And yes, psychology has often used the arts in its studies, just think about how Freud uses literature in *Interpretation of Dreams...* But not just psychology. The link between the arts and science are deeper than we think – and I am thinking physics and mathematics in particular...

But I am digressing... Let's see what the key scientific foundations of body language analysis are, one by one. This may sound a bit theoretical. I promise you that we will start getting "our hands dirty" with practical analysis. But you will need it. You will need it to develop your skills but also to study further if you wish to.

To start with, there is a *regular and steady correspondence between some nonverbal signs and their meaning,* for example:

- *Smiling* – happiness
- *Slouching* – insecurity or physical uneasiness
- *Eye contact* – trust and interest
- *Lack of eye contact* – distrust or lack of interest
- *Looking up* – thinking, taking a pause to think
- *Looking down* – avoiding confrontation and conflict (some may read it as submission, and it may be at times; but the actual core meaning is "I don't want to fight").
- *Lateral eye movement* – often means that you "want to get out" of that conversation or situation.
- *Pupil size can tell us lots of things about internal feelings and states of mind* – a large pupil means you are liking what you're seeing or experiencing, if it squeezes, it means the opposite. Dilated pupils are often also the sign of drug use (both legal and illegal).
- *Stepping back* – taking emotional distance; this may mean disapproval or just the need to have "your space".

The list goes on... For example, there's a whole branch that deals with *hand-shakes*... Talking about which, it may be one of the most important things at interviews. As we are on the topic... Firm but not strong, tight but formal, not "I am with family" warm, like the Pope does and by all means no double hand! The double hand in handshakes shows familiarity, warmth and protection.

To recap, *body language analysis is part of psychology, but it is linked with other sciences and it has its own branches and fields.* Some as specialized as handshakes, or hand gestures, or eye movement!

We will see all these branches as we go along, but for now let's look at two with weird sounding names: *haptics and proxemics*

HAPTICS

I bet few people have ever heard this word in the right context, and it means *"the branch of body language that studies how people touch and what it means".* Of course, touch is a very important part of body language.

Haptics in particular has *strong cultural influences.* Look at the difference between a Japanese person who does not even shake hands and a French guy who kisses his friends (of any sex) every time they meet! The Brits do not like to touch each other, while Italians do it all the time... So, my piece of advice is to be very aware of the cultural baggage people carry with them when you analyze haptics.

Then there are people who are "touchy feely", who like to touch and to be touched, and others who don't. This is a very complex psychological and personal matter. It may depend on many things, including past experiences, upbringing, confidence with your own body etc.

A moment of reflection: you see now that you need anthropology, sociology and psychology (cultural, social and personal factors) to analyze haptics correctly?

And there is a key division here:

- *Touching yourself*
- *Touching others*

When we talk or communicate, *we often touch ourselves. Most of the time we do it involuntarily.* Here are some typical gestures, for example:

- Scratching your head
- Touching your nose
- Rubbing your hands
- Touching your chest
- Scratching your leg

There is a general misconception, and it is that every time you touch yourself when talking you show discomfort or even deceit. No. That's wrong! You may scratch your leg because it is actually itching. Otherwise, for example, it is far more likely to mean uncertainty than deceit.

Rubbing your hands has been taken by movies, drama, and popular culture to describe dishonest merchants who are about to grift you... But that is not the science! That's fantasy! *Rubbing your hands is a sign of excitement.* It usually means anticipation, but sometimes also "Oh good!" the discovery of some good news.

The meaning of *touching your nose* has become part of popular culture too. Ask around and they will tell you that it means "I am telling you a lie"! That is one of those silly simplifications that do not help the reputation of this science!

First and foremost, *never read a nose sign on its own.* With the nose, you *always need other sings to interpret it.*

Secondly, touching your nose is very often a *sign that you do not trust what you hear.* The exact opposite.

Finally, remember that the nose is a very sensitive part of our body and very often we touch it or scratch it just because it is slightly itchy or dry... Don't confuse a cold with a lie!

So far, we can see that there is a huge difference between the actual science of body language analysis and popular beliefs about it...

A very interesting use of haptics body language experts all over the world actually comes from Queen Elizabeth II. It is part of her posture, but have you noticed how she holds her own hands in front of her lap? That has been noted as an impressive sign...

In fact, it isolates her in her position of superiority to anybody else around. Holding hands shows equality, but she cannot be seen as "equal", so she only holds her own hands. Then she gives (shows) her knuckles to the audience. That means "stay off". And it finally resolves a problem for very powerful people: what to do with your hands? They far too often give away your insecurities, fears, subconscious thoughts... This way, no one can "read into the Queen's mind through her hands". It is in fact regarded as one of the most impressive signs of authority.

Compare that with George W. Bush, who often put his hands in his pockets and pushed out his elbows. That hid his hands, and he looked like a peacock trying to look bigger than he actually was... A display of power, for sure, but which to the expert eye showed a huge abyss of insecurity.

The way we touch ourselves gives away great signals about us. And we can develop our own ways to touch ourselves, to look more confident, calm, self-assured, positive etc. But learn from Bush Jr's mistake; it can backfire!

Let's talk about *touching others* now. This is very much influenced by culture and personality, as we said. But apart from this, *the way we touch others depends a lot on how at ease we are with each other.*

For example, body language analysts noticed that very often, at the very beginning of a romantic relationship between people who have not been friends before, there's *indirect touching.* What do we mean by that? We mean that people touch each other's objects, clothes, accessories etc., instead of actual bodies.

It is more often the male partner in a heterosexual pair who moves first and touches an object belonging to the woman. The first actual touch then can make all the difference... If it is the hand, it gives an idea of respect, equality, friendship etc. That would be ideal. And for people who are so inclined personally, it should come naturally.

If the first touch is on the leg, it will very strong sexual signals, and it may show that the person is mainly or only interested sexually. Shoulders are also common as "first place to touch", as touching them may give a sense of protection.

There are so many variables to consider when we look haptics when touching other people.

- Who touches who (first)
- How the other responds
- How long is the contact
- Which part of the body touches which
- How large is the contact surface
- When and why this happens
- Cultural and social factors.

The point is that *touching people is always a matter of social, emotional, interpersonal negotiation.* We all know it from experience. Just think about that most beautiful but often difficult of body contact acts, a hug!

Hugging is a sign of empathy and care basically like no other. You need to be very intimate and at ease with each other for "a good hug". Of course, there are societies where hugging is common, others where it is rare. In some countries, friends hug, in others, especially male friends do not (female friends may do more often, as visible in many social and cultural backgrounds in the USA or GB).

The "Mississippi" count for hugging may not be correct, but it gives the idea of *how much we invest in a hug.* And I am not talking about money, but confidence, intimacy, even "face" (self-confidence).

So, haptics help us understand two things mainly:

1. How people feel about themselves
2. How people feel about each other

And this is just one of the many branches we will see in this book! But let's see another now...

PROXEMICS

Proximity is super important in reading body language. And "proxemics" means the *"study of where people are and how they move in relation to each other".* This includes:

- The distance between people
- The position in relation to one another (left, right, behind, in front etc.).
- The levels people are at (higher, lower, equal)
- The direction people face and turn (towards each other, away from each other)

Imagine two people back to back with their arms crossed... How would you interpret it? That they have had a massive disagreement or row and don't want to talk to each other? You'd be very likely correct.

Imagine two people facing each other. Now imagine if they lean forward, towards each other. Isn't that a sign of "agreement", of mutual interest etc.? And how about if they lean back? That may show "distance", "disagreement" ...

This is why sitting back with your arms crossed at a job interview means losing it. It shows you take a distance from the panel, but also that you're closed to them (arms crossed) and if you also cross your legs then you just show that you are overconfident and "look down on them". And they will "keep in touch" ... yeah trust it!

But proxemics also studies *how we react to each other's positions and movements.* Actors spend a long-time training to react to other actors; it's in fact a core part of learning acting. But on a stage, you will also exaggerate and sometimes ritualize these action-reaction gestures.

In fact, in reality *we tend to "downplay our reactions" in real life.* This becomes more so in formal situations. If you are at the pub or bar with friends, it is far more likely that your gestures and movements will be much bigger, much "grander" and much more dramatic than during a meeting with your boss! At least we hope so...

"What is more difficult," you may ask, "reading proxemics in formal or informal situations?" The honest answer is that in formal situations, proxemic signs (and other verbal signs) are smaller, "downsized", if I can use this word. On the other hand, fewer things happen; there isn't much "background noise" to pick up the signals.

The opposite is true, and it depends on how formal or informal situations are. From a simple informal meeting between acquaintances and a full-on stag party on one side, and from a simple fairly informal office meeting to being knighted by the Queen of England on the other...

The fact is that *the more informal the situation is, the more people feel disinhibited and free to move and gesticulate etc.* But if gestures and facial expressions become clearer, more definite and "bigger", so does the "background noise" caused by other people moving, talking loudly, gesticulating etc.…

Both have their difficulties. *In formal situations, you will have to focus on details. In informal situations, you will have to exclude all that disturbs your focus.*

Having said this, let's see some *core principles of proxemic action-reaction.* Let's take 3 examples to illustrate them.

1. John and Sheila are sitting facing each other. John leans with his chest towards Sheila and she *mirrors it*; she leans with her chest towards him too.
2. John and Sheila are sitting facing each other. John leans with his chest towards Sheila and she leans back with her chest, still facing him.
3. John and Sheila are sitting facing each other. John leans with his chest towards Sheila and she turns sideways away from him, so that she is no longer facing him.

These are simple everyday situations that you must have witnessed many times in your life... But now I am asking you to look at them from the perspective of a body language analyst...

In case (a), we have the action known as *mirroring*. This always expresses *accord, empathy, agreement, appreciation, and even, in some cases, physical attraction or love.* In this case, whatever is going on between John and Sheila, we know that they are "on the same page".

Mirroring, be aware, is often used by charlatans and grifters to gain your trust, so now you know it...

In case (b), Sheila does not mirror what John does. Instead she *neutralizes it.* She basically does not allow him to close their distance. She keeps the same distance by moving back. This is a sign of *diffidence, discord, disagreement, mistrust or simple insecurity and uncertainty.*

Finally, in case (c), Sheila actually *breaks away*. She basically "gets out of the physical dynamics with John". She literally "exits" their proxemic relation... A bit like leaving a meeting halfway through, or a party if you prefer... In this case, *Sheila is subtracting herself from John's authority.* She is not showing simply disagreement: *she is rebelling, claiming her freedom.*

Like there is rarely a sudden switch between "love" and "hate" or "friends" and "enemies" in real life, so there is rarely a sudden change from mirroring to braking away in proxemics. When it happens, it all looks so visible and dramatic. Like in those old Hollywood movies when an old authoritarian aunt would suddenly turn her back on her niece's suitor and walk off with a grand gesture...

It does happen, but it is rare. People usually move from mirroring to mirroring less, then to neutralizing softly and with garb, then more, then intently, and only if that fails people start breaking away. And even here, first partially and only then fully.

Observe when people meet in the streets and one wants to leave... You will first see movements going back, claiming distance. Then a little step to the side. Then a bigger one, then the chest turns. This is actually often mirrored by the other person most of the times. Otherwise, the thing gets embarrassing as one is holding the other behind, being "insistent" or "sticky"...

In many cases, using proxemics to signal these things is understood subconsciously by others and the whole process becomes consensual... It almost looks like a parting ritual we all understand... But we actually do it without even being aware of it...

So, keep in mind there are three key action-reaction principles and in fact, yet again, observe them in the people you meet every day. At the office, you may find out things that had escaped you for months... Maybe that there are "feelings" between two colleagues (or that the "feelings" are long gone) or that your boss (or teacher) favors someone (mirroring gives it away very often).

And now we can move to a practical chapter... I want to show you some of the key rules and even "tricks of the trade" of body language analysis. And we are going to do it right now!

3

THE BASICS OF BODY LANGUAGE
ANALYSIS

Frowning, scowling, sighing, ogling, scratching, slouching... The list of words we have for body language is huge... Why? Put simply, there are loads of expressions in body language. But can we try and make some sense out of this huge language system we so often ignore? Yes, we can. And this is exactly what we are going to do.

Let's start with a little experiment... Think about your favorite teacher at school. Picture him or her in front of you, by the whiteboard (or blackboard if you are my generation!) Done? Keep the image in mind. Now, we all had teachers we couldn't stand the sight of (the voice of etc.). Pick your least favorite teacher ever.

Done? Great... Now, draw the contours of the two images you have in mind. Just pretend you have a big marker and draw their silhouettes. If your least favorite came out as one of those chalk shapes police people draw on the street in movies, then you really didn't like him! Jokes aside, overlap them...

I bet they had different postures... Am I right? Of course, because studies show that the thing students remember most about their schoolteachers is their "antics", like their weird posture, original body language, facial expressions, strange habits of tone of voice. Not the actual words, not the actual lessons...

But if you compare the two postures of the two teachers, one will give you a positive impression, the other a negative one. You see, you already "read" their body language. And you kept all this knowledge in your subconscious until now. And with a simple analysis, you now have a rational understanding of their body language (or part of it).

This exercise tells us a lot about body language. For example:

- We pick it up even if we are not aware of it.
- We react to it even if we don't know we are actually reacting to it.
- It influences our opinion of people.
- We remember it for a very long time. Longer than we remember words, in fact!
- People give off body language signs all the time.
- Some signs are positive, and others are negative.

Reading body language is like opening a book full of secrets. That book has been on the shelf for years, and we have not picked it up... It's time we did it now...

POSITIVE AND NEGATIVE BODY LANGUAGE

Let's start from a basic distinction. *Positive and negative body language.* And we will do it with a little experiment... Tell me, of these two, which one is positive, and which one is negative?

a. Punching your fist on the table
b. Smiling

Of course, you will agree that (a), "punching your fist on the table" is negative while (b), "smiling is positive. But now let's add a few more...

c. Frowning
d. Touching your nose
e. Tapping your foot
f. Leaning backwards on a chair

Now things become a bit less straightforward, don't they? You may think that frowning is on the whole negative, but not as negative as punching your fist on the table. And I would agree. This tells us that there are *levels of negativity and positivity in body language.*

Negativity and positivity are on a cline, on a gradient, from very negative to very positive. In between, you have 'quite a lot negative/positive", "a little negative/positive" and all the grades in between you wish to use...

I can hear your question, don't worry, "Is there neutral body language?" Great question actually!

The idea of *neutral body language* is interesting for me... Let me tell you why. By neutral body language we mean "relaxed" and "at ease". So, in body language "neutral" is actually "positive"! I think it tells us a lot about the real meaning of life... But maybe this is something we will discuss in a philosophy book...

Now, back to positive and negative. What makes us measure negativity in body language? I mean, which attitude makes body language negative? There are a few:

- *Aggression*: of course, aggressive behavior makes body language negative.
- *Hostility*: it may be less overtly expressed than aggression. So, it will be more difficult to detect. But it really makes a huge difference if you can spot hostility on those you have in front of you...
- *Emotional distance:* this often translates into physical distance, as we will see.
- *Diffidence and lack of trust:* it is related to emotional distance and it can be its cause, but it's not the same. A friend may feel a lot for you but not trust you on some points. And yes, you can understand it from your friend's body language.
- *Disinterest:* this may not be as negative as outright hostility or aggression, but it is still negative and finding out about it will save you a lot of disappointments in life...

These are different "types" of negativity, or better different "sources" of negativity.

So, what you need to do when you spot general negativity in someone's body language, is to *work out which of these emotions or attitudes it expresses*. Understanding that your interviewer at a job interview is disinterested will tell you a lot about your prospects of getting a job. You know when you get home from a job interview and they ask you, "How did it go?" You usually give an impression, then waste days in anxiety... How about if you could actually tell rationally that it didn't go well because you read it in the panel's body language? Less anxiety, less disappointment, more time to move to your next interview...

You see, people nowadays often have a bad attitude about "knowing the negative" ... It's a sociological matter. Society has become so difficult and frustrating that as a defense mechanism many of us prefer "simply not to know." But if you know it rationally beforehand, you will not get the emotional blow when the news is broken to you.

Emotionally, being told something negative by someone in a position of power or knowing it beforehand is hugely different. The second immunizes you from disappointment, frustration, loss of face. And it gives you more time and energy to dedicate to your next move.

Let's pause for a little *reflection*. As a pedagogue, in fact, I have to tell you that a good learner is a reflective learner. So, every now and then we will pause and think back a bit... Have you noticed that *you have already started analyzing body language?* Analyzing means "breaking into parts" ...

So, what we can say about *analyzing body language is that we need to understand what the attitude is (emotion, thought etc.) behind nonverbal signs.*

And we can start with three steps:

1. *Divide between positive and negative.*
2. *Decide the level or degree of positivity and negativity.*
3. *Identify the core attitude behind the sign, gesture etc.*

It is a bit like mind reading, yes... Honest mind reading though...

"But how about the positive?" I can hear you! Talking about mind reading... Okay, I kept it last to end on a positive note.

Here again, of course there are *levels of positivity.* From "enthusiastic", "enamored" or "ecstatic" to "lukewarm" and "not fully hostile" ...

But *what causes a positive body language sign? What are the attitudes behind it?* Here they are:

- *Empathy:* this is by far the overriding attitude or feeling behind all positivity. When people understand what you feel, whether you are expressing a problem or expressing joy, they will open up both emotionally and physically (with body language).
- *Trust:* if people trust you, you will see it in the way they sit, move, smile, speak, look... And this is very important... Think grifters and what they may know about our body language! We'll come back to this... Trust me (I love puns!)
- *Interest:* if people are interested in what you say they will show an openness and positivity about your ideas, feelings etc. through their bodies.
- *Agreement:* it is not the same as interest. Understanding agreement through body language puts you a step ahead.
- *Relaxation:* you can't imagine how being relaxed changes your body language. Of all the attitudes (states of mind) that influence body language relaxation is "the big switch". You see, if you empathize, trust, agree etc.... you are relaxed! If you feel aggression etc. you are not! It's like "the bedrock of all positive attitudes". Or the consequence of them all? Let's say both.
- *Confidence:* we will have to look at this in detail, because there is a key difference between overconfidence (which is aggressive) and real confidence (which is protective). People who are positively confident have a warm, mother or father like body language. Overconfident people have an "army general" type of body language...

If you know which signs project positivity, you can do two things with it:

- You can *learn to read positive signs.* So, you will know when your teacher or boss *actually* agrees with you.
- You can *learn to project positive signs.* And this is as life changing as it gets. People who project positive signs have better lives: they have more respect and esteem, they are more trusted, they are happier, they receive more information (yes, people talk openly to positive people), they have a better life experience and even better career prospects.

Now we have made lots of progress. But there is much more to say.

BODY LANGUAGE IN CONTEXT

Let's take an example from verbal language and linguistics. Look at this statement in two contexts:

1. "What a nice day!" (The Sun is shining and it's hot).
2. "What a nice day!" (It's pouring down, it is cold and miserable).

The sentence is the same, but the *meaning is the exact opposite.* The second statement is ironic. And we cannot understand irony without some form of context. Yet irony changes the meaning of statements to their exact opposite!

As we do with verbal language, *we need the context to understand body language. We need contextual information.* But what is context exactly?

Context is everything that "comes with" a sign, which can be immediate (near and clear) or even very remote. It can actually be another nonverbal sign.

Imagine children coming back home all dirty and muddy. At the door the mother is waiting for them and you see:

- She has her fists on her hips, akimbo.
- She is tapping her foot.

What do you understand from this?

Your *first reading* would tell you that she is angry, that she has a scolding attitude and posture, very authoritative and even impatient.

But now I want to show you the mother's face: and she has a beaming smile!

The smile is contextual to the other two signs. And now you understand that she too is actually playing with the children. How often do we do it to "pretend scold"? It is actually an important social and educational activity. I won't get into the details, but for example it plays down the role of severe punisher-parents often have; it teaches children that even that is a role, not something parents like doing, showing self-irony etc.... Beautiful!

But for what we need to learn, there is a key point: *your analysis is only as accurate as the completeness of the sings and contextual signs you collect.*

It is a bit like "playing detective", like Columbo, for example... You need to collect a lot of data, in fact as much as you can and then piece the puzzle back together.

So, we can agree that *you should absolutely never interpret a body language sign in isolation. Read them all together, as different letters of the same word, or words in a sentence...* None alone can give you the full meaning.

If the smile is another nonverbal signal, and it is immediate context, now forget you ever saw it. But now I will give you another piece of information: *you know the mother's mindset and cultural values and you know that she does not care that her children get dirty. Actually, she values children's freedom and contact with nature above all.*

This is a very important piece of information which changes the whole perspective, once again. *We do not live in a cultural vacuum.* Personal, social, family, and culture and even traditions affect all we do and express.

Let's look at it this way. When you don't understand someone, very often you go to a friend of his/hers to get a "final interpretation". The "trust me s/he didn't mean it" from someone who knows him/her well... Why? That sentence is based on knowing the context, which includes the history of the person and his/her values...

"Hold on," you may be thinking, "I can't know everybody's past!" You are right, and you will not need it most of the time. If you are trying to find out if that shop assistant is trying to fleece you, then you won't need it.

But this is to show you how far we can go with the data we use, and how important the context may be. Still, with the shop assistant, you will want to take into consideration other contextual factors as well, for example:

- Is this a reputable shop?
- Have you shopped there before?
- Are you a regular customer?
- Is the shop assistant permanent or just filling in for one day?
- Do you know the shop assistant from outside this shop?

Like when you read a book you may need to know about the times it is set in, the culture it comes from etc.... the same will apply to analyzing body language.

CONTEXT AND AMBIGUITY OF BODY LANGUAGE

At the beginning of this chapter we looked at a list of nonverbal signs, remember? We started with "punching your fist on the table" and "smiling" (assuming with a real smile!) These two are pretty *unambiguous.* A bit like the words "good" and "bad", "love" and "hatred", "happiness" and "pain".

But then we added "frowning", "tapping your foot", "touching your nose" and "leaning back on a chair". And these are not unambiguous, in fact, they can be *very ambiguous out of context and on their own.*

Tapping your foot with music means that you are feeling at ease and "getting into it". Tapping your foot without may be a sign of nerves (or maybe that you have a tune in your head?) Tapping your foot while standing may be a sign of disapproval, but sitting may be a sign of boredom.

So, if it is a formal meeting and you tap your foot under the chair... I'd bet you are bored... But if you are standing and staring at someone or at a particular place, I would think you are showing disapproval and impatience...

In this case, *you need the context to resolve the ambiguity of the nonverbal signal.*

Frowning can be a sign of perplexity but also of concern... If you are telling a friend that you had a bad experience and you see a frown on his or her head, you'd assume that s/he is expressing empathy, an honest concern about your happiness, health etc....

If you give in your homework and your teacher frowns – well, that can't be positive now!

Here again, it is the *context that tells us how to interpret a nonverbal sign.*

Everything happens in context. As a body language reader that makes all the difference. For example, in a *formal context* people will be stiffer, less expansive, less expressive. And this means that *body language becomes:*

- More controlled and less spontaneous
- More limited (smaller gestures, smaller movements, less expressive facial expressions)
- Slower and more predictable (there is like a "script" to follow in formal situations)

In short, our body language changes according to the situation:

- where we are
- why we are there
- who we are with

And this is all part of the context.

BODY LANGUAGE AS A HOLISTIC PRACTICE

Let's go back to our foot tapping mother. We started from her foot and ended up to a conclusive reading only after seeing her face... That says a lot about how we read body language. You see, it is not "foot language" or "elbow language" for a reason. *We read the whole body, as a continuous and coherent expressive body.*

There are *specific branches of body language analysis for face, position and distance, hands etc.... even for eyes...* And we will see them very soon indeed! But the meaning comes only after looking at all the signs a person gives off and then putting them together. It's like reading a book... You don't just read verbs, or only adjectives or only nouns, do you?

"But is there a direction, an order? Where do I need to start from?" you ask quite correctly... No there isn't. But there is a professional trick I will teach you in a second.

Most times, *and most body language readers are caught by particular movements or gestures*, exactly like everybody else does. So, the foot tapping of the woman will very likely be the first thing a professional and an amateur body language reader would notice.

This is simply because *there are very visible gestures, expressions and movements that stand out.* It's a bit like shouting or raising your voice or laughing in verbal communication. You cannot fail to notice these signs.

The difference is that while everybody notices it, the expert body language reader "activates".

Let me explain this to you. What would you do, with your very eyes, if you saw someone punching the air? You would *zoom in on the strange, eye-catching and anomalous gesture, movement or facial expression,* right? That's the most natural thing to do. In fact, it's unconscious, spontaneous, it's a reflex, an instinctive reaction.

Now let me tell you what a professional body language reader would do... *She or he would zoom out from the strange, eye-catching and anomalous gesture, movement or facial expression.* The exact opposite, and that's what I mean by activate.

Why? How can you see signs from the rest of the body if you zoom in on a little detail? It's like people who play sports like basketball... They keep an eye on the ball but keep their peripheral vision on teammates and adversaries... They are trained to do it. Or while you focus on the ball, someone can steal it from you...

So, this is a bit of an insider secret, a trick of the trade, but I wanted you to know it. This way, you can start with the right tools, means, habits and attitude you need to become very proficient.

And the very first exercise I will ask you to do is just this. Go out (when you have to, don't rush out just because of this!) Go where there are people, maybe when you go shopping or you are going to school or work...

Okay? As you are out, look at people around you. If they move, some particular movement or gesture will catch your attention. Instead of zooming in though, "activate" and zoom out ready to catch any other signs his or her body gives off.

And after you have done this, we can meet again for the next Chapter, where we will learn about the very nature of body language, why we react the way we do...

4

WHY DOES THE BODY REACT THE WAY IT DOES?

BODY LANGUAGE

Booooooo! Did I make you jump? Probably not because you're just reading this. But if I had shouted it from behind your back... The question is, why do we jump when someone scares us?

It is a reflex, and a very visible one. Like when the doctor tries your reflex with the little hammer (or gavel) on your knee. You cannot avoid it. In this case, the heart itself "skips a beat" (metaphorically, it beats faster actually). When the heart is affected, the whole body responds. You feel an adrenaline rush. Your mind suddenly resets and goes into defense mode. Your nerves and muscles stiffen. Sometimes even bladders have reactions...

This is a glaring example that *we are not fully in control of our physical actions and reactions.*

But how about if similar but much smaller, less visible episodes happened to you all the time? You don't consciously look away when someone irritates you most of the time, do you? You *can do it*, just to *show your disapproval.* But even if you don't want to show it, your body will.

In fact, *our body tends to respond to almost any experience and even any emotion we have.* And this is where *natural body language comes from.* If you're happy, you smile. If you're angry you scowl. If you're nervous your body stiffens etc.

"But how about actors and politicians," you're asking? We could spend hours talking about the long tradition of "looking at how the body communicates to then reproduce it as naturally as possible". In a way, the *ability to reproduce seemingly natural body language* is one of the things that makes an actor convincing. Centuries ago they had ritualized and exaggerated gestures no one would take as natural. At the times of Shakespeare, actors did not want to "look real". Then things changed and this art was perfected.

And of course charlatans, grifters and politicians jumped on the gravy train and learned how to use *recitation body language.* This is a form of *acquired body language* which is very conscious and intentional.

And in the middle? Is *recitation body language* the whole of *acquired body language?* No, not at all actually! We pick up body language unconsciously all the time. There is a theory in language studies called *Accommodation Theory.* It means that when we like someone, we imitate their language (tone, choice of words, even accent), but also their nonverbal communication (like body language) ... The opposite happens when we do not like someone we are talking with.

This happens all the time and for sure you have found yourself using "the words of a friend", meaning her or his typical language. We actually notice string relationships because people start "talking the same and moving the same" ...

So, in your own personal body language there is a *cultural inheritance* you carry with you. That facial expression from your beloved relative, that gesture from your old friendship group... all these signs you picked up along the way will surface every now and then subconsciously.

So, we have seen that there are at least three types of body language:

1. *Natural body language*
2. *Acquired body language*
3. *Recitation body language*

We go back to the nature vs. nurture debate... Well, in the end it turned out to be more practical and less academic than we thought!

UNDERSTANDING WHAT THE BODY IS TELLING YOU

Now that you know that body language has different origins, you can start making a distinction. Let's take a practical example... Imagine you are a professional body language analyst. Imagine there's a famous politician on TV and she is making a big speech. Imagine they ask you to analyze the speech to find out "what she is hiding"...

Fine, now, you will need to find out:

• What she wants you to believe.
• What she actually feels about what she says.
• If there are any cultural interference that confuses the reading.

Her body is telling you all these things at the same time. And it's your task to tell them apart.

If you have seen professionals at work, maybe you noticed that often they say things like, "He used his hand this way but at the same time he frowned..." Finding *contradicting signs* is actually a door into deception. Not necessarily, don't take me wrong. There are *no ultimate absolutes with human sciences*. We are not machines.

But you see, *reading signs in conjunction can give us a clue whether the person feels consistently with what he is communicating or not.*

And how about the body language that is culturally acquired? Sometimes, it can give us the sympathy for or affiliation to a cultural group. Rappers are a clear example. Their hand gestures really tell us "I belong to the rapping cultural tradition", with all its links to urban, Black etc. communities.

The way people cross legs in the UK can tell you if they come from the upper class or the lower class... Allow me a cultural reference... Have you ever seen the TV series *The Jeffersons,* with a fantastic Sherman Hemsley as the unforgettable George Jefferson? Do you remember his iconic stride? What did it tell you? He told all the viewers that he was "deeply proud to be a member of the Black community".

When you read body language you then come home with three different sets of information about the person:

- *His or her cultural background.* This may be relevant according to what he or she is saying, or, in some cases, you may need to remove these signs as "noise" because they confuse your assessment. For example, if someone is selling you a vacuum cleaner you may want to focus on whether it is a con instead...
- *What he or she wants you to believe.* Finding out which gestures and nonverbal signs were "planted" there to convince you gives you a great advantage. Note though... It does not mean that if someone is "acting" they are also lying. The politician in question will of course use his or her body language training... The point is finding out if *his or her body is telling a different story from his or her lips.*
- *What the body involuntarily says.* Which, of course, will confirm or disprove what the person is saying.

This is very important when racing body language... In many cases, it is a bit like "cleaning out everything" till you can actually see the truth... And in many cases, it is a lot of cleaning! But it isn't always like that.

We looked at a big and important example. Actually, if people understood every time politicians lie to them, we would be much better off...

But at other times you may want to *read body language to help the person.* Psychologists do it all the time. If you are breaking a piece of bad news to someone, you can't expect the person to respond honestly all the time...

There may be many reasons for this:

- The person is in shock.
- You are not in a relationship of confidence.
- The person may not want to upset you with his or her pain...

If you have to break bad news to someone, always look at their body language. They may be in much more need of help than they actually admit. Any sign of *closure*, especially in front of their chest and stomach, is actually a sign of extreme pain in these moments. Your friend needs comforting.

Slouching or bending forward is a bad sign too... Your friend may be giving up, or literally "felling the weight of the situation"...

The worst sign, however, may just be the blank stare and expressionless face. That is a sign of emotional shock...

Yet again, the context is all important in these situations. You may even expect a fairly string and detached reaction when a doctor gives a patient bad news. This is why it should not be the doctor that gives it, but a psychologist... But if it happens in a friendly relationship, you should expect a request for help in the body language. Even a hug...

HUMAN REFLEX, INEVITABLE OR NOT?

Some people are like marble statues though. They never seem to give off any unwanted signs. Maybe the most impressive of all in this is our old acquaintance the Queen of England. It may look like it is possible to *control human reflex and unconscious body language totally.*

In this case, of course it would be very hard to find out lying and cheating. But is it really possible? The answer is yes... and no!

Yes, it is possible to control natural reflexes. No, it is not possible to control them completely.

In fact, great part of the body language that politicians (and actors) go through involves not expressing nonverbal signals, but repressing them. "Getting into character" means "becoming a blank slate" and that involves calming down the body to a point where it does not have to express itself non-verbally.

Actors and actresses do it all the time. Luckily, most politicians and insurance agents are not that good at acting. But they still train to avoid spontaneous body language.

To do this, you need a trainer that checks on how you move, gesticulate etc. and then tells you to "stop this and stop that" till it becomes easy and then second nature for you to hide your body language.

But no one can do it perfectly and all the time. There are some obstacles to this:

- *Some areas of body language are harder to hide, some impossible. Eyes especially cannot be easily controlled and faces too.*
- *It requires an effort and energy to hide your natural body language. People can do it for a short time but not all the time.*
- *Sudden and unexpected events can suddenly bring out natural body language.*

In fact, political speeches are almost always, filmed at a distance, short and controlled, there is no sudden "boo!"

Look at the Queen again. She has been training for this all her life... But still you will rarely see close ups of her, and rarely when she is giving a speech. Her appearances are very short. Everything is under control all the time.

Having said this, I want to give you a tip... Imagine you are in the middle of a transaction with a guy who really hides his natural body language well... What can you do?

- You can tire him out if you have time. This way, his defenses and energy will drop, and natural body language will resurface.
- You can *surprise him.* No need to go "boo!" but a sudden and unexpected gesture, sentence, proposal etc. And be ready to read his body language immediately after you surprise him...

THE HUMAN BODY

Reading body language also means focusing on different parts of the body at the same time. Think about it; it is not easy to read feet and eyes simultaneously. That's why, first of all, *you should keep at a decent distance when reading body language.* This is also because if you are very close to the person you are analyzing, you will literally be interfering into his or her body language. You don't read body language on elevators…

So, where can you stand?

- You should not be too far, because you need to see the person's eyes.
- You shouldn't be too near, because you need to see the whole body and let the person feel safe.
- You should not even be directly in front if in person. You may become the person's focus.
- About 10 feet away slightly to the left or right (about 30°) is fine.

Now you know where to position yourself, shall we have a look at some key areas of body language analysis? These all look like technical words, and they are. But we will explain them in simple terms, and you will learn the basics of these fields.

KINESICS

Kinesics is the study of movement within body language. We don't just communicate when standing, with facial expressions and gestures. *We also communicate through movements.*

The way you walk, the way you run, when and where you go… Which way you turn… There are so many aspects of movement that the list could go on for days. We have also seen that kinetics is important in proxemics (how we stand and move in relation to each other). All the different fields of body language analysis are linked, of course.

But let's look at some core elements of kinesics…

- *The direction of movement.* Which way does the movement go? Does it go towards someone or away from someone? Or maybe something?
- *The speed of movement.* Running away is not the same as walking away. And walking away slowly is not the same as walking away in a hurry.
- *The size of the movement.* Walking totally out of the room is a clear sign that you intend to finish an interaction, even peacefully... Instead, just stepping away may mean that you want to stop the interaction, but not just yet. How far you move does matter, of course.
- *The accentuation of the movement.* By this we mean how big, theatrical, exaggerated etc. the movement is. And this can show either intention (if the person wants to make a dramatic gesture) when intended, but total lack of control if it is natural.
- *The complexity of the movement.* Simply walking is not the same as walking and jumping, or walking and waving, or walking and shaking your head. We need to analyze movements in all their complexity.

To these, of course we need to add the different types of movements, like:

- Walking
- Sitting down, squatting etc.
- Standing up
- Moving hands (waving etc.)
- Moving arms
- Head movements

The list is long... An interesting one, for example, is crossing your legs. This can be a sign of ease, a cultural sign, or even a sign of discomfort according to how you do it.

It is a sign of ease because you lift a foot from the ground. You are less "grounded". Usually, when we feel unsafe, we want to feel in touch with the ground as much as possible.

It can be a cultural sign. Just think about the difference between resting your ankle on your knee, a sign of great confidence, often used by men and even frowned upon when women do it in some cultures. Now compare with aligning the knees one on top of the other. In Britain it is common but among middle- and upper-class men and all women. Working class men do not use it often...

It can be a sign of distress, especially if the lifted foot tends to drape back onto the other leg. This is quite a common sign by women especially, and it shows that the woman is "closing up completely", even that she feels sexually threatened, or at least that she wants to cut off the sexual sphere from the encounter.

Always keep an eye out for how people move, and you will find out much more than you may imagine...

OCULESICS

Talking about keeping an eye out, *oculesics is that branch of body language analysis that studies eye movements.* It is actually a sub-field of kinesics. You know that eyes move, but have you ever actually observed them? They move all the time!

Of course, their movement is limited in space (unless you count eye focus as well), but there are many other things to look out for in eye movement:

- The direction
- If it is repeated, constant
- Linearity (eyes can rotate, for example)
- The length of the movement
- The focus

Taking the last first, there are two key *directions of focus:*

- Inside focus
- Outside focus

Think about it carefully and you will notice that when people look "inside themselves" or outside, you can notice the difference. An outside focus is piercing, an inside focus is vanishing.

Then again, where someone focuses one's sight is of course very important. The famous looking at a watch during a (romantic) meeting says it all. But also, the frequency of *focus shift* is important. If you are out on a romantic date and you look at someone else once, your partner may not notice it, pay no attention to it or forgive you. Start doing it a bit more often and I am not sure your date will end up in a "happily ever after' scenario...

Everybody changes focus every now and then. But doing it constantly shows *interest in someone or something.*

While we are here, I will tell you an acting secret... Actors always look *above the heads of the audience.* So do good teachers... Why? They have to avoid *eye contact,* which is far too powerful to hold especially if you are, in a manner of speak, telling a story, a "lie" of sorts... You will find it hard to stay in character and loom at the audience in their eyes.

So, sometimes even in a very frank and honest conversation, people look away, they change focus. But that is just like "taking a break, a breath". Sustaining eye contact is very hard indeed.

On this topic, no... If you can stare at someone in the eyes for three second you are not necessarily in love with each other. Another urban myth about body language we have to dispel.

Let's see some typical eye movements.

- Looking up. This may mean many things. From desperation, to the fact that you are thinking, disbelief, confusion etc.
- Looking down. This usually shows disappointment and a will to avoid eye contact. It may also show shame and lack of self-confidence.
- Looking sideways briefly. That is usually a way to take a small break, maybe to think or reflect.
- Looking sideways intently. That is usually a sign that the person is actually very interesting in someone or something else.
- Repeated lateral movement. This is usually a sign that the person is trying to get away from this interaction.

And here is possibly the biggest urban myth we have to dispel. No... eyes up and left does not mean someone is telling the truth and eyes up and right does not mean the person is lying... It's been debunked and proved wrong by actual research... Sorry it is not that easy.

The *key to understanding if someone is lying is to find a contradiction between what someone says and what his or her body says.* There is no "one tell-tale sign" of lying... And we will see this in the next chapter.

The *sequence of shifts instead is important.* Let's go back to our romantic dinner which didn't start too well. Jack caught Rose look away at the other table, and not at the food... There's a very good-looking man over there...

Now, Jack gets worried and it does not happen anymore... Of course Jack may think it was a chance.

Next scenario, Rose looks that way once more... If before she did not know there was a good-looking man, now she shows that she liked the surprise... or at least this may be what Jack thinks.

But how about if Jack catches her eye as she is looking over at the man on the other table?

Imagine she moves her eyes and looks at Jack straight in his eyes...

Now imagine she shifts her eyes to the other side first, then down on the table and only later she looks into Jack's eyes?

You will agree that in the first case, we can be quite sure that Rose has "nothing to hide". But her behavior, actually the sequence of eye shifts in the second case leaves us bug doubts about it. Doubts which we will have to investigate, as body language analysts.

We have seen two important sub-fields of body language analysis which you can add to the two we have seen already: haptics and proxemics.

These four fields together will give you a good framework to work with.

Of course there are specific fields, for all the different parts of the body, and we will come across them soon enough.

Before we move onto the next chapter, where we will learn to interpret body language in the light of what people say and what their bodies tell us, let's recap and see how many areas (branches) of body language analysis you know so far.

- *Haptics* – which studies "how people touch" themselves and others.
- *Proxemics* – which studies "how people stand and move in relation to each other."
- *Kinesics* – which studies "how people move".
- *Oculesics* – which studies "eye movements".

Keep these in mind because you will need them next, when we actually get to the chapter you have been waiting for... the one on detecting lies!

5

IS WHAT HE'S SAYING THE SAME AS WHAT HE'S ACTUALLY DOING?

Mayla gets home from her new job. She starts talking to her husband about her first day at work, but she gets the impression that he's not paying attention, so she says:

"Are you listening Chris?"

And he replies, "Yes, of course, Mayla, I'm all ears," looking out of the window...

You get the point. What Chris says does not match what his body language is saying. Beware, this is not a clue to jump to conclusions. But it is a *"gap between two realities we need to investigate"*. See yourself primarily as an investigator, not a judge. And in any case, the value of a judgement depends on the accuracy of the investigation.

In this chapter, we will focus on this gap (or lack of) ... We will look at different ways of communicating and what discrepancies can tell us about the real meaning behind the words (and behind gestures too).

HOW HUMANS COMMUNICATE

Look at Michelangelo's *David*. Watch Leonardo's *Mona Lisa*. Listen to Beethoven's *9th Symphony*. Read a novel or watch a play by Shakespeare...

These are all forms of communication. Written words, spoken words, even the weird noises we make are communication. But so are lines, colors, shade, perspective in paintings. And so are notes, beat, tempo in music... In cinematic language, zooming, cutting, close ups, photography, the soundtrack... they are all ways of communicating.

Communication is far more than a grammar book of any language! It is true, however, that we *humans heavily rely on verbal communication.* Much more than other animals. For example, fish communicate with colors and movements very often. Some birds communicate by singing, others by displaying their feathers or even doing ritual dances... Other animals are very verbal, on the other hand (cats, dolphins, elephants, whales etc.).

And dancing may be a very good example to use. Think about dancing. Think about how *you dance. Most of us, see, live and use dance as a way of expressing ourselves freely.* Most of us don't do the splits; most of us don't plié, sauté etc... We dance spontaneously and naturally.

But if you dance regularly, soon you will learn maybe to waltz, or to twist, or to rock 'n' roll (that's actually hard) or to tango (hard too!) Then if you progress you move to figurative tango etc.... Of course, to be a ballet dancer you need to start learning all those moves when you are a child

But what does this tell us? It tells us that we naturally communicate through dance. But the more we learn about it, the more we become experienced and then even professional, the more we learn "new signs", new "words" new "units of communication" as well as new styles etc.... We can express more because we have more tools.

And this is true of art, singing, acting... all forms of communication in fact! Think about it. You may not be a great singer, but we can all hum a tune (even off key, okay) when we are happy. No, you may not be as great a singer as Aretha Franklin or Natalie Dessay. But they had a massive natural talent and they studied and practiced!

Similarly, you will never paint as well as Leonardo or Caravaggio, but you can do simple drawings. And the more you practiced painting, the more you equipped yourself with "painting words", "painting phrases" etc....

You see, plants even communicate through smells. And some animals understand that language. We too understand if something is good to eat or not from its smell. So, that is another form of communication, but in our case it's only passive. Meaning we receive it, we "read" it. Well, some people may "speak it" too in what they think is a funny situation...

What matters is that *when we say "language" most of us mean "verbal language" but there are loads of languages we "read and speak" all the time, each with its structure, its "words".*

These languages, or ways of expression, can be divided into *visual and auditory*, mainly. We Humans have fairly good sight (and we depend on it more than all other senses), and below average hearing (it's good, but it does not match that of most mammals). Sharks also have the ability to detect electromagnetism, a sense we apparently do not have... Dogs have an incredible sense of smell...

What it tells us is that *our main means of communication depend on our best developed senses.* Cats for example have impressive hearing and they communicate even at frequencies we cannot hear (like dolphins). Dogs only communicate visually at close range, because their eyesight is poor, but wolves howl to speak to other wolves miles and miles away. We can't do that, and our sense of hearing is much weaker than theirs...

How many ways do humans use to communicate? The list is huge, but it is mainly divided into visual and auditory:

Visual languages:

- Painting
- Sculpture
- Written words
- Visual symbolism
- Mathematic signs (they are a form of communication)
- Dancing
- Body language

Auditory:

- Spoken words
- Music
- Singing
- Whistling

Then, we also have *forms of communication that mix visual and auditory,* like:

- The theatre
- The cinema
- The opera
- Ballet
- Many concerts nowadays, since Madonna transformed concerts to a mainly auditory experience to a visual and auditory one.

Finally, *some forms of communication also have a kinesthetic nature.* This means that they use *body movements and gestures to express ideas, feelings etc.* For example:

- Drama
- Dance and ballet
- Opera
- Miming
- Juggling and similar arts
- Skateboarding, synchronized swimming
- Body language!

And we have come full circle.

All these have a mean of communication (hands, feet, movement, oil on canvas, sound etc.) and then a code, which is a series of meanings and then a "grammar" to put together these meanings.

EXCHANGING INFORMATION WITH VERBAL COMMUNICATION

Is verbal language exceptional? Yes and no. No, it is not at all unique to humans, as we believed only a few years ago. We mentioned dolphins, but even closer to home, cats use a verbal language (they actually use 6 different verbal languages!) with clear meanings and quite expressive indeed.

Yes, it is because *we use verbal language as our main form of rational expression*. This does not mean that we cannot use verbal language for irrational communication... When you read or write a poem, a novel, or sing a song, you are actually expressing, in many cases, emotions, not ideas... But to express irrational concepts, in verbal language we need things like imagery, metaphors, similes etc.... We need "figurative" or metaphorical language.

What's more, *our society places a lot of importance on verbal language.* Peace treaties are written in words, not painted nor expressed through ballet. Similarly, laws are written on paper and signed. They are not presented as a statue nor as a symphony...

But there is more; *verbal language is at the core of education and it is taught extensively.* We mainly *learn through words* (books, discussions, presentations) and we *learn a lot about verbal communication.* Think about how long you spent learning English in your formal education and how long you spent learning music? Drama? Art (usually a tiny bit more)? Ballet? Body language? Never even heard of at school.

Now I will ask you to wind back a moment... What did we say about dancing? That the more you learn about it and the more you practice it, the more you become proficient. This means that:

- *You can express more concepts and with more precision.*
- *You have more control over what you express.*

This is the reason why most of us *prefer verbal language: we can control what we say very well.* We take it for granted but think about how a child speaks.

They don't control what they say as well as we do. They start picking it up from family members, then they learn it at school etc....

This is a double-edged sword... On the one hand, it allows us to communicate with confidence and great precision. On the other hand, people who are very skilled at it may hide their true intentions...

This is why sales agents are all very good at speaking and verbal communication. They have the "gift of the glib". And if they don't have it by nature, they learned it!

This very point shows us *why learning nonverbal communication is very important:* we are not balanced. We need to look at "the other side of communication" which is often ignored, but which can also show things and intentions which are easily masked with verbal communication.

PAYING ATTENTION TO NON-VERBAL COMMUNICATION

Of all the forms of non-verbal communication, the *most common is body language.* Not everybody paints, not everybody dances, not everybody sings. Everybody uses body language. Similarly, even painters, dancers and singers aren't always painting, dancing or singing. But *we (and they) use body language all the time, whether we (they) want it or not!*

But there is more.... When singers are singing, when dancers are dancing, when artists are painting, they know exactly what they are doing... *they are in control of their communication. With body language, in most cases, people are not in control of what they are saying.*

We often listen and look away (like Chris did in the example at the beginning of this Chapter). Mayla, on the other hand, was paying attention to Chris's body language. This is why she had "the impression that he was not listening". And this is why she is unlikely to believe that he is "all ears".

Did we say at the very beginning of this book that women, statistically, pay more attention to non-verbal communication? It is not a mistake that women, on average, have better EQs (emotional quotient, like the IQ but for emotional

intelligence). *Just paying attention to body language and non-verbal commu-*
nication stimulates your emotional intelligence.

NON-VERBAL COMMUNICATION AND LIE DETECTING

But I know what you are thinking... "How do we actually find out if someone is
lying to us?"

Good. Let's debunk myths first. I said it but I will repeat it: *there is no one tell*
sign that tells you someone is lying. Those are myths about body language
analysis. However, do not despair, because...

There is a method, a procedure to find out if someone is likely lying or telling
the truth.

To start with, notice the "likely". We said that body language is used by detectives. True, as evidence, to find clues etc. Not as definite proof. This is not
because it is not scientific. It is because we simply cannot be inside people's
minds. And there may always be a reason for gestures etc., that we cannot see...

So, what is this method? First of all, it uses *both rational and irrational*
thinking and communication. You should never draw a conclusion on an
"impression". But you should let impressions come into your analysis. You see
the trick?

These are the core elements:

1. *Listen very carefully to what people are saying.*
2. *Watch carefully all the non-verbal signals they give off while saying*
   it (this usually happens at the same time, but with recordings we can
   change it).
3. *Match, overlap what they say with their body language.*
4. *Eliminate noise* (cultural signs etc.)
5. *Find inconsistencies between words and body language, between*
   verbal and nonverbal language.
6. *Analyze the probability that the person may be lying.*

These are the key steps. You have learned and are learning quite a few details and techniques about the first five steps. As to the 6th, which is where you draw all the observations you have made together, we need to add some information.

Think about body language as someone bouncing on a mattress. The mattress is your subconscious. We react to it through non-verbal communication. However, the subconscious is never really steady. It's like a water mattress in continuous movement.

In a way, a bit of "waving, undulating, bouncing" is continuous and very normal. We are never on safe firm land psychologically speaking. At any "wave" we have a lack of balance in body language. That may result in a facial expression, movement, eye movement etc. These are usually small, because they come from small waves.

But they also have a certain regularity because these waves are sort of regular. A sudden wave, however, will cause a sudden non-verbal sign. And that is what you want to detect in particular.

The fact is that when we lie and we know we are, we "disturb the waves of our subconscious". It's like we drop a heavy weight on the water mattress... You see, the movement of the lie inside our person upsets the subconscious which reacts by pushing us off balance causing a dis-harmonic nonverbal sign.

Or, for another comparison, imagine you are reading a seismographer... You need to detect the odd peak in the line...

Once you detect the peak, the odd wave etc.... you need to go back to what the person has just said and analyse her or his body language in detail (easier with recordings).

Here, verbal language becomes again very important. *Can the actual sentence be a lie?* If the person said, "Good morning," it's far more likely that the sudden nonverbal signal is due to a stomach cramp than a lie...

Also *look at repeated patterns.* If a person behaves like there's been a bigger than usual bounce in the water mattress *(almost) every time s/he mentions a certain topic, then there is a clear emotional problem with that topic,* and you may well be on to something.

Yes, it is, on the whole, far easier to find out a lie if the person has to talk for longer... And this may come in handy, because very often, swindlers talk to us for a long time trying to convince us. And in this case, just show that you are not convinced and force them to keep talking, so you can find the telling pattern of unusual body language. That would be enough evidence to reasonably suspect a lie.

AVOIDING MISCOMMUNICATION

But there are positive applications of verbal and nonverbal communication studies as well. We have already said that learning to control your body language, in an honest and moderate way, is actually very good for you.

Let's jump back onto the water mattress. You see, our subconscious can get into "patterns of waves" that produce repeated patterns of gestures we often are unaware of, and at times, we cannot control. To one extreme, we have nervous tics, on the other, we have less visible, small movements that, however, other people notice (more or less consciously) and sometimes they clash with what we intend to communicate.

Let's get practical. Imagine you have the tendency to rub your hands unconsciously. It's a very, very common habitual gesture. In fact, it may even come from a need for safety, solace, protection. However, also because magazines have made a huge disservice to our science, most people see it as a sign of dishonesty.

Trust me, no sales representative will ever be successful with this hand rubbing habit!

Let's take another common example. Feet pointing inward. It tends to project lack of confidence and a desire to protect oneself. But it can also be just habitual posture. Now imagine having to take on an authoritative role, like being a teacher, or a parent who has to give rules to children... Be sure that the children in both cases will need lots of convincing... Even with a good tone of voice etc. *that mismatch will stick in the children's minds and contradict what you say.*

These are all examples of *miscommunication. Being aware and correcting your body language can avoid miscommunication.* You should not, and you cannot, change all your body language. You should focus on one or two habitual signs that have caused you problems in the past. Slouching is a major example of this.

But being aware of body language also avoids other, maybe worse, miscommunication events. An example... This is something teachers in multicultural countries know or should know. Some communities, in particular the Black Caribbean community, you do not stare at someone you are not friends with. Eye contact has to be short and you need to move away, or you will be seen as aggressive.

Do you know how many times teachers have thought that students if this community "are rude", "don't care about what I say" or "never listen" simply because they associate eye contact with interest?

Similarly, when the teacher stares at the students in the eyes, do you know how many students from this community feel that the teacher is "being a pain", or "challenging me?"

Just knowing about body language allows you to get on well with many people and avoid sometimes really unpleasant misunderstandings. And changing this or that habit can make a huge difference to how well you can express your messages to others.

And now, get ready for a couple of very practical and straightforward chapters. The next for example, will look at all the different parts of body and how they speak.

6

READING BODY MOVEMENTS

We couldn't possibly write a book on body language without looking at all *the different parts of the body and how they communicate.* It's a bit like reading different parts of a sentence. Each body part has its own characteristics, its own way of speaking. They also have different limitations. For example, you can't move your head as far as you move your legs and feet. And you can't move your feet as well as you move your hands... There are physiological differences.

But there is more... some body parts tend to communicate certain thought processes or feelings, while other body parts are better for another set of feelings and thoughts. At the same time, even cultural factors influence how we use body parts. We have seen it with hands and handshakes.

Last, but not at all least, *some body parts are easier to control than others.*

Let's compare these:

- Eyes
- Mouth
- Feet
- Arms

Which ones are easier to control? Which ones are more difficult?

You may end up with a list of arms – feet – mouth – eyes from easier to most difficult and for the average person, you would be correct. But there are differences between people. Some people can even move their ears! I can move my scalp... And how about those who have prehensile feet?

Feet in fact show us that we can learn to use and control parts of our body that we would not expect to. People who paint with their feet (or their mouths) are a shiningly beautiful proof of it.

But we will talk about feet in a moment. For now, we shall start with the top... the head.

HEAD AND FACE

We are very conscious of our head and face. Most of us imagine our "essence" to be placed somewhere in our head. That's where we "feel" we are thinking, watching, listening etc.... It's the center of our focus, basically.

Ironically though, *we hardly control our facial expressions at all.* Mind you, we can, and we try very often. We "pull faces"; we "wear smiles"; we "make faces" etc. But to the expert eye, eyes, ears, eyebrows, lips, nose and even facial muscles always give away much more than we think.

It is also true that we focus on people's faces when talking. So, this means that *people are aware that their faces are "under scrutiny".* And this means another thing for the skilled body language analysis... That if someone wants to hide a non-verbal expression, most likely that will be on his or her face.

Let's put it like this. If you know you are lying, and you know people are staring at your face, you will try to control your facial body language... It makes sense...

But every time a person tries to control and repress a natural nonverbal signal, expert body language analysis can notice it. It's like stopping twitch... You need energy to do it, you need to stiffen your muscles... It's never completely successful.

Head

Your *head tilt* is important. Think about students daydreaming at school. They tilt their heads very often. This does not mean that they are not paying attention. It means that they are relaxed and creative.

In fact, *head tilt left or right* usually shows relaxation, comfort and even deep mental processing.

A *head leaning back*, instead, is a sign of disconnection, usually caused by deep frustration or total exhaustion. It often means something like "I can't bear this anymore." But beware, this does not need to be what we think. In a lesson "this" may be a personal thought, a family problem, an emotional disappointment. It does not have to be your lesson!

A *head leaning forward and down* can mean many things, from shame, to feeling guilt, to feeling tired. Sometimes it is a simple way of avoiding eye contact (often fixing the eyes on hands, feet etc.)

A *head leaning forward but straight ahead* is usually a sign of great interest, but it can also be used ironically, especially by young people, meaning "Okay, now, you see how much I listen?" but in a challenging, even mocking fashion. This last sign is usually accompanied by eyes open in an exaggerated way.

Eyes

They say that "your eyes are the window of your soul" and there is far more than commonplace in this. For example, did you know that your eyes are in fact physically part of your brain? Yes, we look at each other's brains all the time. Sorry if I left you with a weird picture.

And our eyes are by far the most difficult parts of our body to control. Try not to blink! Impossible. Try staring at someone into his or her eyes for long; you will have to move away at some stage... Try keeping your focus fixed on a single point for long... It gets hard... But above all, try hiding your feelings... Eyes speak, and they do it independently from us.

So, let's see some of the most important signals our eyes give off...

- *Dilated pupils* express interest, pleasure, even sexual or emotional attraction.

- *Shrunk pupils* show dislike, even repulsion.
- *Eyes up* usually show thinking and doubt.
- *Eyes up right or left* usually indicate visualization. This does not mean "lying"; it means that you are using your visual brain, even to recall real facts in a visual way, like remembering your primary school friend's face.
- *Eyes sideways left or right* usually denotes attention to what you are hearing, attention to your auditory sense.
- *Eyes down right* usually show you are having an internal dialogue.
- *Eyes down left* usually show that you are checking facts.
- *Eyes down* shows you are focusing on your sense of smell.
- *Eyes shifting left and right* usually means "I want to get out of this"; the person feels embarrassed, not at ease, or wants to leave.
- *Eyes shifting in different directions* are rare, and they show great confusion most of the time, even panic.

Now, don't take these as "hard and fast rules". To start with, always keep in mind the option that someone is following a fly. This is a silly example, but with a serious message. There are external factors that catch our attention all the time. It may be a light, a flower etc.... People do not have any obligation to stare at you straight all the time...

But there is more to eyes than where they move... There is of course the expression. Sadness, joy, worry, concern, fear, care etc. all appear in the expression of our eyes.

This may be difficult to explain in few words, also because eyes, their shapes and their overall expressive qualities vary from person to person (actually from eye to eye as no two eyes are the same, even on the same face!) But all research shows that we all recognize the feelings and emotions expressed by eyes very easily.

In fact, this was used as evidence for the argument that body language is natural, because everybody can recognize eye expression "naturally". Okay, that was again a bit of the nature vs. nurture debate. But hey, I told you it went on, and on... and on again...

Eyebrows

Did you know that we tend to look at eyebrows very carefully when talking to people? Those two hairy lines under our forehead are one of the main focal points we have... Thinking about it is funny because we don't think much of eyebrows...

Perhaps we subconsciously know that eyebrows are a very important area for body language... They tell us if a person is happy, angry, confused etc. To read them, divide each eyebrow into two parts:

1. *Inner eyebrow* (the part towards the center of the face)
2. *Outer eyebrow* (the part towards the temples)

On the whole, it is the inner eyebrow that leads the movement of the outer eyebrow. So, focus on this part and check out for:

- *Raised inner eyebrows*: that shows openness. It is often interpreted as a sign pf honesty and trustworthiness. But it can also mean interest and the fact that the person is trusting you or what you are saying.
- *Lowered outer eyebrows:* this usually shows sadness, pain, suffering.
- *Lowered inner eyebrows:* this usually shows anger, or at least frustration.
- *Whole eyebrow raised:* instead of being led by inner or outer eyebrow, this movement is led by the central part of the eyebrow. Here the eyebrows form arches with the center part being the highest. This shows surprise or astonishment.
- *Whole eyebrow straightens and lightly lifts.* In this case, when you see two eyebrows raising lightly but becoming straight, it means the person is excited.
- *Eyebrows pulled together:* this happens when we pull them both in the middle above our nose, and it usually shows confusion, or at least an attempt to understand what you are hearing, seeing etc.
- *Slightly raised eyebrows together with half open mouth (with flattened lips) and a stiff brow* usually means fear.

There are lots of things to read on eyebrows, as on people's mouths, and we'll see it next.

Mouth

The mouth is a very expressive part of our body, not just because we use it to speak... It is also, note, an opening into our inside, and as such it has a very intimate function.

- *Flattened lips:* this is a very clear sign of tension, nervousness, or worry. Do note, however, that lips also flatten when we are tired. A good body language reader knows when her or his colleague has had a bad night.
- *Full, plump and relaxed lips:* this is of course a sign of relaxation and ease. Note that you need to adapt this concept to the actual natural shape of the person's lips. Some have naturally plumper lips. But they all change.
- *Pouting lips:* this is actually a very innocent sign. It does send us back to our childhood. However, many people know that this is a sign of physical attraction. The fact is that because you "drop your defenses", it may actually mean that you find the person attractive.
- *Lip biting* is one of the most noticeable signs. It shows that the person is in trouble, or perceives danger or conflict... This is one of those gestures politicians are told to avoid at all costs.
- *Partly open mouth showing top teeth (incisive teeth):* this is a sign of relaxation, attraction and interest.
- *Higher lip distorted with one side raised higher than the other:* this is a sign of disgust or great disapproval.
- *Broad smile showing teeth:* usually the upper teeth show more than the lower ones, but it may depend on the mouth's shape. This is outright joy and happiness. But it is also a sign of approval. How many smiles by teachers have shown students that they are on the right path?

But here we need to make an important point. *Always look at the sides, the tips of the lips.* People are quite aware of the function of mouth body language. This is because they are easy to read but also for the reason we said before: they are a very intimate part of our body and one often under scrutiny.

So... many people have learned to fake their mouth body language. But there is a problem... The "fakery" shows up at the very tips of the lips. It's a physiological thing. When you are lying your muscles tighten.

So...

- *Relaxed tips of the lips:* this goes with positive expressions and it shows that they are genuine.
- *Tense tips of the lips:* this goes with negative expressions. With a positive one, you may wish to question whether it was genuine or not.
- *Tips of the lips pointing up:* real smile.
- *Tips of the lips pointing down:* disgust or fake smile.

Go quite safe with the up and down tips... There's basically consensus on these two particular signs.

Breathing

This action involves our head (nose and mouth), chest and even belly. Belly breathing is a little trick I would suggest you learn if you don't do it yet. It is much more relaxing than chest breathing. We use it when we sleep. Singers use it, actors use it... But does breathing tell us about a person's inner thoughts and emotions?

Breathing is such a vital function that it really goes deep as body language meaning. To start with, notice that breathing is both:

- Spontaneous
- Controlled, voluntary

When we stop controlling our breathing the natural "autopilot mode" steps in immediately. What an amazing gift we have! Or sometimes, the "autopilot" takes over without our consent because we receive a shock, a surprise, we worry, we lose energy etc.

And this is exactly what you have to do:

- *Check for sudden or even slow changes in breathing patterns.*
- *Check for unusual breathing.*

To be precise, use these two parameters:

- *Slow breathing means relaxation* (confidence, lack of worry etc.)
- *Fast breathing means excitement or worry, tension, fear etc.* Keep these two separate. Excitement can be positive. Your breathing becomes fast also when your partner proposes to you, or you to your partner!

However, in many formal situations (meeting at work, or dealing with an insurance agent, giving a speech...) the idea is that you will project confidence if you have a slow, well-paced and relaxed breathing pattern.

And going back to the beginning, you see why learning belly breathing can make a huge difference in your life? You can control your breathing so much better with belly breathing. Really, just try it!

Shoulders

Shoulders do not move that much, but when they do, you can't miss them! The metaphorical meanings of shoulders (strength, support, confidence, stamina etc.) are basically the same as their overall body language message of this part of our body. Soldiers wear their rank on their shoulders, kings and queens wear ermine, managers in the 80s went crazy for shoulder pads because they made them look more "bossy".

Read shoulder movements in two main directions:

- *Shoulders out and back:* the person feels safe, confident, strong or/and calm, in control.
- *Shoulders in, forward and slouched:* these show lack of strength, tiredness, a sense of having lost, lack of confidence and of control.
- Careful though, *shoulders that look excessively and unnaturally*

raised can project arrogance.

They are such a big and visible part of our body that we cannot hide them. So, do be careful about what your shoulders say about you.

Arms

Arms are very mobile parts of our body. This means that they have a great expressive range or potential. But there are some very important characteristics of arms:

- They are one of *the parts of our body we are most in control of.* Very often arms say what we want them to say, rather than what we actually mean. But not always.
- Arms are often *used to "take possession of the space around us".* In this, they play an important role in power games, hierarchy etc.
- The *size of arm movements and gestures is very important.* This may change culturally (shall we mention Italy again?) but it is also a sign of *how confident, how in control and how much you think of yourself.* People who think they are bosses have often very broad arm movements.

Arms can even be threatening, as they are a primary fighting tool. Then again, which *type or arm movement we see* is also important. Thus...

- *Moving arms close to your sides especially turned inward, towards the center of your body:* this is a sign of discomfort, even fear. It is an attempt to defend yourself and at the same time to "make yourself small" and less visible.
- *Folding your arms* projects confidence but it also closes channels with the person you are talking to. You defend yourself and distance yourself. It's a "no" ...
- *Arms that open sideways* can have different meanings. Especially with palms forward or at times upward, they can be a protective sign, while with fists or downward palms they may be menacing or a way of taking control of space.

- *Arms upward* are a sign of freedom, joy and release.
- *Arms behind your back* is a rare occurrence nowadays. It was a favorite position of army, navy etc. officers. I have also seen dukes, bishops and prelates use this, even Popes... They actually project authority and self-confidence, especially when walking. Having said this, they hide your hands, so, many people may not like it. The position here is that where you have an arm stretched down behind you and you hold it with your hand at about elbow level.
- *Swinging arms when walking* is a sign of well-being, confidence and freedom. Excessive swinging though may look funny and clumsy and even indicate the opposite, lack of confidence. It really is a flexible sign and a lot will depend on the context.
- *Elbows out and hands in pockets or on hips,* as we have seen, is a way of making yourself look bigger. A sign that the person wants to take a controlling position but at the same time it shows weakness and insecurity.
- *Hands on hips or in pockets and hands forming V shapes backward,* basically when your elbows point backward is another disappearing gesture, but it shows openness and at the same time a "submissive" or at least very non-confrontational attitude. It's always been more common among young people, especially men, possibly as a "social marker", meaning they do not occupy a dominant role in society.

What matters most is that you look at the *quality of arm movements.*

- *Fast arm movements* often indicate confusion, stress and lack of control (not always though).
- *Powerful arm movements* can show aggression an engrossed person.
- *Calm and controlled arm movements* show, well, calm and control.
- *Exaggerated arm movements* are rare in most situations. That's because we know they would give away our lack of control and that is exactly what they tell us when they happen.
- *Sudden clumsiness in arm movements* shows that something has gone wrong in the person's perspective: doubt, uncertainty, maybe even fear or concern.

Hands and Fingers

Hands are likely the most communicative part of our body outside our face. We use them to give rational signals, codes, indicate, explain, count, greet... But there are some key hand movements that can give the right or the wrong impression about ourselves...

- *Hiding hands* is a bad sign. It gives the impression we are hiding something. Sometimes this is true, but it may just be that the person is shy or embarrassed, or even worried for that matter. Never hide your hands at job interviews!
- *Front or back of hands.* This is a huge difference. Your *palms show openness.* When we want to mean "I swear", what do we do? We raise our hands and show our palms. On the contrary, *the back of your hands shows closure.* It means "keep away" and showing you knuckles in particular is a sign of aggression.

Here I need to tell you a story. A real one. Do you remember Tony Blair? He was noted by body language experts for always "waving his knuckles" at the audience during speeches. He also had very big hands, and the effect was even bigger. In any case, this was seen as both defensive (but accepted) and as a sign of strength. Even of dishonesty, maybe, but overall the audience read it as "confidence".

Not a pleasant gesture but wait till the next and short-lived UK Prime Minister came along... Gordon Brown too showed the back of his hands in speeches but in a lower position than Blair. Blair was actually "in your face" with his hands (surprise pun!) Brown seemed uncomfortable with his own hands... And people read it as? Weakness first of all, and a touch of dishonesty too.

This shows that really, *the way these movements happen, in a qualitative way, makes all the difference.*

- *Fists* are always an aggressive sign when shown to other people. The more towards the face they point and go, the more aggressive they are. But also waving them, pretend punching etc., matter, as well as facial expressions. But fists by the side of your body with arms stretched down show rebelliousness, or that the person is trying to control her or his anger or strong emotions.

- *Raising a fist in the air* is voluntary body language and it simply means solidarity with those you are with. From there, it was then taken by socialism and communism, with the left hand, as a greeting.

- *Raised open and hand in extended arm* is another voluntary sign and it means "obedience". The Nazi and fascist salute are all forms of submission... In fact, look at how Hitler used it... ever noticed that he never showed his palm to his subordinates as they did to him? That floppy hand of his ended up showing his palm upwards... to the sky... He owed loyalty to none of them... only to the "cause" is what his salute symbolized.

- *Palms of your hands attached to your body* mean that you are keeping calm, or even that you are protecting yourself.

- *Palms of your hands touching, joint* can have a lot of meanings. They don't necessarily mean "I beg you". The fact is that this position opens up an energy bridge inside your body. So, it may be a sign that someone is restoring his or her energy circulation, that the person is at peace with him or herself. Or it may just mean that the person is thinking in earnest about what you are saying.

- *Scratching your palms* is often (not always) a sign of confusion, discomfort or uncertainty. But remember, it could always be physical itching!

- *Palms up on the table, knees etc.* is an extreme sign of honesty and collaboration.

- *Palms down on the table, knees etc.* is instead a sign of control and it may denote that the person does not want you to know something.

Lots of things we can say with our hands, and still we have not seen them together with fingers!

With fingers, first of all, look if they are *relaxed, so bending slightly or tense, which means that they are either stretched out straight or in a fist.* A sudden tensing of the fingers of a person is a clear sign that something isn't quite right... Then of course, we have to look at how we move and position our fingers.

- *Pointing at people* can be a necessity but, in many cases, pointing at the person we are talking to is aggressive especially with a straight finger.
- *Pointing with a soft, arching finger* especially at things is often misunderstood. People may think it means "lack of character", "sloppiness" and "weakness". On the contrary it is often a sign of very strong and deeply rooted self-awareness and self-confidence. The fact is that pointing is always a way of establishing a relationship. The soft finger is *protective and respectful* towards the pointed thing or person. It is a *sing of confident kindness*, which we often mistake for weakness.
- *Playing with the ring*, whether you are wearing it or not, is actually a sign of distress most times. It's a way of touching yourself to reassure yourself.
- *Little finger stretched out sideways* either means that the person is a piano player or... that s/he feels very at ease. That finger feels vulnerable, doesn't it? So, exposing it like that means that you feel perfectly safe.
- *Fingers touching forming a ring* too may have a lot of different meanings, mainly positive like connectivity, interest, deep thought or looking for a solution.
- *Nail touching and scratching* can be a sign of embarrassment, disagreement, doubt, discomfort or just boredom...
- *Checking your fingernails* is now rare in important situations. Why? It's so clear that you are not paying attention. And it does mean that, or, worse, that you are but you disagree or even that you think what you are hearing is total nonsense! Again, avoid it in a job interview...

Even fingers, you see, say lots of things about us.

Legs and Feet

... and we need to add legs and feet to complete the list... On a general note, we are *less aware of our legs and feet than we are of hands and arms.* Because they are "down there", because they are often out of sight (under tables etc.) they tend to get forgotten quite easily.

At the same time, hands and feet body language is very much influenced by culture. The US "feet on the desk" may cost you your job in some countries, while they project authority and relaxation in the States... Arabs point with their feet and showing the sole of your foot is an insult. The same in some Asian countries.

In some countries, crossing your legs with the whole leg draped over the other is a "feminine" sign, and men avoid it. In others it is perfectly okay with their masculinity (or perceived masculinity). In many countries still nowadays women who open their legs when they are sitting are frowned upon. Still, let's get some general guidelines.

- *Legs open, apart* show confidence, self-control and at times relaxation.
- *Knees tight together* show lack of confidence even a perceived threat.
- *Crossed legs* too show a sense of informality, willingness to relax.
- *If the foot wraps on the calf* it may show a perceived threat, even sexual, or total closure, as we have said already.
- *Swinging leg while crossed* can be a sign of total ease, even happiness or, if nervous, it may show restlessness.
- *Legs lightly apart when standing, with feet forward* means self-assurance, self-control and calm. This is the singing position, the one professional singers use because it is relaxing.
- *Legs tight together, especially with feet together or point inward when standing* indicate a strong lack of confidence or sense of being unsafe.
- *One foot forward one pointing sideways when talking or standing* is quite common and it shows a certain level of arrogance, of determination, but not always. In any case it points to the idea that the person is interpreting the meeting, event, moment as a transactional situation... Basically it's business and not a social experience for him or her. In fact, you will often see it in speeches, conferences, lectures and presentations...
- *Feet up* is of course always a sign of relaxation and ease.
- *Feet backwards when sitting,* especially if "grabbing the leg of the chair" often show worrying or discomfort. This is very often

accompanied by a leaning forward position of the upper body. This is not a dishonest person; this is a struggling person who needs help, but s/he is ready to collaborate fully and even go the extra mile.

- *Shaking foot* is always a sing of restlessness, but note that some people do it all the time and they are almost incapable of stopping it. In this case, they are more likely very nervous by nature.
- *Touching feet when talking*, usually when sitting and often with crossed legs. You must have seen people touching their feet in these situations. This is a sign of introversion… The person is internalizing what s/he is hearing or looking inward, not outward.
- *Crossed feet at the ankle* depend a bit on the situation. If at home and relaxed it's just a sign of relaxation. If it is during a discussion, meeting etc., it may show closure. Maybe the person is refusing to accept what s/he is hearing. Look at other signs in the body to make sure (folding arms, inner eyebrows lowered etc.).

Once more, always check if the movements look:

- Natural/unnatural or contrived
- Relaxed/tense
- Proportionate/exaggerated
- Controlled/out of control
- Friendly/aggressive
- "Going with the flow"/sudden and out of place.

Do this with legs and feet but also with all parts of the body and you will soon get a very good reference framework to analyze people quite deeply…

In fact, take a stroll in the park and look at how people move their bodies… Make a mental note… At first divide between positive and negative, then try to add the actual emotions and attitudes that their bodies are revealing to you.

You could do it before you move on to the next chapter. In fact, if in this chapter we have used cubism, by which I mean that we have broken down the human body into its components, in the next we will use an impressionist perspective. What do I mean? You are going to find out right now…

7

SEEING BODY LANGUAGE AS A WHOLE

A cubist painting breaks the different parts of the body and places each on a flat plane for you to see. But it does make it hard to see the whole body, to give an overall reading of the general picture. We stressed very early on the importance to read the body in a holistic way, as a whole. And this is what I meant by "impressionist reading". Look at a Monet painting and you will get a general impression while the details are not well defined. But they do make sense as part of the whole.

So, without further ado, we shall now get out of our artistic metaphor and see what you need to look at a person's body as a whole. Now we will look at how posture is part of body language, different types of posture, we will go back to where you should stand in relation to the person and to a link between verbal and non-verbal language. Ready?

EXPRESSING WITH BODY POSTURE

Posture in itself is hard to define, isn't it? It's "the way one stands" but also "the way one moves". It is broad and general, much more like an "impression" than a detailed and specific element. But you do know, for example, that many people decide just with posture if they are going to like someone? We also recognize people without seeing them well, in the shade etc. and we use posture to do this.

This tells us that we are very aware of posture, and we use it to make very big decisions, including the "like/not like", "trust/not trust" and "beautiful/ugly" ones. But we do it without being fully conscious of it. And this is why at the beginning of the book I begged you to correct your slouch if you have one. People see it, they do not rationalize it and yet act upon it very strongly.

General though it is, we can categorize body posture along *broad lines*. One such lines is the distinction between *dynamic posture* and *static posture.* Let's start with the latter.

Static posture

Static is quite easy to understand. It means that it does not move or, more broadly, tends not to move. The Queen has a very static posture, to go back to the most analyzed person in body language all over the world. Very often, people in a position of power and in a formal setting (a speech etc.) have a very static posture.

It tends to project *authority, confidence* and even *reliability.* A person who does not move, or moves very little is fine when standing on a stage, behind a desk, in front of a camera… It's not a good posture to keep when you are mixing with friends, interacting with people etc.

And then there is the *degree of how static you are.* Very static postures end up looking "stiff". Not everybody can carry the super static posture of the Queen of England successfully. Even US Presidents tend to be more fluid, less "stuffy". They move slowly, but they do, even in formal speeches. The Queen does not even blink and even when she is walking, she makes it look like she is not moving at all…

Dynamic posture

A dynamic posture is one where the person tends to move. This does not mean "walk" (it may), it means move legs, shoulders, head, arms etc. Here too, it all depends on the *context and the degree.* Moving too much may be good for some comedians just because it looks funny. Politicians will not move too much, nor will medical doctors, nor will sales agents...

You see, a *dynamic posture* projects a *lively personality,* a *likable* one, a *friendly* one, and even a *healthy one.* This is also why US Presidents tend to be more dynamic than monarchs like the Queen or the Emperor of Japan. They have to be liked, and they also need to prove they are healthy all the time.

At the same time, it all depends on the situation. If you are dancing... I don't need to finish the sentence. If you are playing with children, having fun with your friends etc. you want to be dynamic. If you are at a job interview, you want to be more static.

When the posture is *far too dynamic,* and especially if the movements do not look coordinated, you give the impression of being out of control, and sometimes this may well be the case. As usual, use other clues to confirm your suspicion (tone of voice, facial expression etc.).

Dynamic and static postures

Here too, we talk about a gradient with many levels. From someone who is dancing around in an ecstatic and free fashion to someone who does not move at all. But I wanted to look at a special category here: teachers. Good teachers manage this very well. They have to move, you see, otherwise their students would fall asleep (or would not wake up!) On the other hand, they have to project authority, so they also have to offer some static postures to the class.

They change very well from one to the other... For example, they will be static when they need to talk to the whole class then become relaxed and dynamic when they walk around the desks to check on the students' progress.

FORMS OF POSTURE

Another quality of posture is what "form" it takes. By this, we mean how *open, inviting, welcoming and non-confrontational* you are on the one hand (*open posture*) or on the contrary how *closed, defensive or even aggressive* you are (*closed posture*).

This too goes on a cline with many gradients. From a person holding arms out ready to embrace to the child clasping his knees while sitting on the ground with his head between his legs.

That last position, you see, closes the whole world off. There is no way to "enter" the child's space, and the child is only showing non vulnerable parts of his body: his shoulders, legs, back and feet. He is hiding his face, his belly, his palms and the inside of his legs. At the same time, the child is looking "within his own body shape".

In between, you can have the person with arms open but not yet ready to embrace, the person with arms folded and legs crossed... There is a potential infinity of positions we can take.

Again, context is very important. If the posture matches the context and situation, then fine. A manager facing a hostile board of directors, a politician who needs to criticize (attack) his adversaries etc. will *need a closed posture*.

Conversely, wishing your grandmother happy birthday with a closed posture will raise some important questions about your attitude, feelings, state of mind etc.

To analyze postures, I suggest you look at children and parents. There is a reason for this... They often quarrel. It's part of growing up. Parents have to be friends and at the same time severe educators, even punishers if necessary. This means that their relationship is in continuous swing between closed and open postures.

Go to the kid's corner of the local park. Look at all the parents and children on the slides and swings and in the sand pits... Look around and find those who are being "friends" and those who are being "naughty child and angry parent" by just looking at their postures.

HOW FAR SHOULD WE BE?

We already said about 10 feet away and not in front, but at a slight angle (30 degrees or so), but is this a general rule? Yes and no. It is a general rule but with two provisos:

- That you can take that position.
- That you can observe properly and hear properly.

Let's see what this actually means... Imagine you are at a party... There is loud music and lots of people... Can you stand ten feet away? You can, but you won't hear anything, and you won't even see much with all the people walking by... or dancing... or spilling drinks...

Similarly, you go to a speech by a very famous politician. There she is, on the stage... then there is a barrier, and security and the first rows of course are all taken... Goodbye ten feet, welcome 100 feet if you are lucky!

Let's see another example. The person you are analyzing whispers. I don't mean that she or he whispers once... I mean that s/he does it all the time... What's the point in listening at that distance?

You are on a busy road... You are watching the person in a video... There are so many different situations.

So, we need to be very flexible but keep in mind these guidelines:

- Make sure you *see well, both the whole body and even small parts of it.*
- Make sure you *hear well.*
- Make sure *you are not top visible.* You should be a *discreet presence.*

So, the 10 feet 30° to one side rule gives you the ideal distance and position in the ideal situation. Be flexible. 15 feet makes no real difference if the acoustics and visuals are good. Don't stand too close, always give the person space to feel at ease.

And it you have to stay far... try to be at least within hearing distance and get a good vantage point.

PS: don't wear red if possible...

LISTENING CLOSELY

Body language is "reading" but it is also "listening". "But listening has to do with words," you may argue. And you would be right – but not fully right. I know, I like puzzling you…

When you analyze a person's body language, of course you need to know what this person is saying. This you already know. But you also need to check for signals which are not just verbal… They are that step detached from being verbal and yet they come with the voice, with words and from our mouth.

Everything that accompanies a spoken word adds meaning to the word itself. So, pay great attention to:

- Intonation
- Volume
- Tone of voice
- Overall delivery
- Pauses
- Interruptions
- Anacolutha (it's when a person changes sentence or thought halfway through, the singular is anacoluthon and it is "something like – actually no" or "I took the car – I was going to…" They always show a change of mind or subject. It may be totally innocuous and proper, but sometimes this hides nuggets of gold for the body language analyst!)
- The formality of the words and tone chosen
- Even the person's accent may tell you a lot.

I'll give you an example with accents. People often use two accents, one is local, or of a particular community and the other is more standard and formal. Not everybody. However, imagine a person choosing to use his or her local accent when talking to someone from outside? It's a sign that the outsider is not very welcome, not very respected. And the more that accent is exaggerated the more it would show hostility. It's like saying, "We are not similar, we are not the same!" This, of course, assuming the person could use a more standard accent.

Also be aware of *non-verbal sound signals*, like little grunts, "mms" (when people agree), "ers", "tut-tuts", "eh-ehs" and of course laughter and giggles... All these are often far less controlled than the actual words they come with.

These offer a very good insight into what the person feels about the conversation and the person they are talking to. These also show you where the person wants the conversation to go. You can see if they want to change subject, or insist on a topic, for example.

We have gone a long way in what feels like a very short, and I hope enjoyable time. Next, we will dive very deep indeed. So deep that we will go under the skin of the person we analyze... Yes, I am teasing you – but it's sort of true!

8

HUMAN BEHAVIOR AND THE MOTIONS OF THE BODY

D id I say that body language analysis is a bit like mind reading? Well, not literally. The truth is that it's more like "reading behavior" than the actual mind... You see, we don't hear the words that the person is actually thinking. That would be mind reading – I suppose. Instead, we are after particular behaviors and the reasons behind them. This is why I said we would be going "beyond" in this chapter.

IT'S A HUMAN REFLEX!

Imagine you are driving along a busy road. Imagine you have a small head-on collision with another car. What do you do? I know it does not look related but bear with me... To start with, your car would physically bounce back. Next, you would switch into "defense mode" straight away... Third, you would immediately consider the other driver as a potential adversary (in psychology we say "position"... you *position* a person in a social role, e.g. as a buyer, as a client, as a friend etc.).

Ok, now let's change road... You are by bike now (bike, not motorbike!) and you are riding down a green road with trees on both sides... Someone comes up to you on the side and smiles... How would you position this smiling rider now?

For sure you would not "bounce back". Secondly, you would open up to this person.

And now I will tell you a secret: they were the same person! Okay, let's abandon our vehicle metaphor now. Society is like this: in some situations, it puts us into a conflictual relationship from the start. Shop assistants and call center operators know it quite well: sometimes clients come with a complaint and the clash is inevitable. Other times, especially when we are free from worries and engagements, we can meet "side by side" and start on a different and positive foot.

Basically, society is the biggest "positioner in our lives". But let's focus on your reaction in these two cases... Why did you react in two different ways? In a way, your car explains it very well. If you bump into another car, your vehicle will recoil and bounce back. The very same dynamics are at play with social relationships.

Let's wind back a few chapters now and recall what we said about job interviews: the panel usually decides within 30 to 60 seconds. What does it mean? That it is during or just after the first encounter (a clash or a meeting of roads?) that we form *first impressions.*

I know, there are people who swear that their first impressions are always right. People make all sorts of claims, though. Instead, let's see what the actual science says...

To start with, that we form first impressions much faster than we actually thought. No, you don't even have those 30 seconds at job interviews. In fact, the speed we have in judging others is *counted in milliseconds!* It's not a typo. On average, we react to a facial expression (note the body language) in *between 33 and 100 milliseconds.* This has been found by psychologists at NY University J.K. South Palomares and A.W. Young in a study called 'Facial First Impressions of Partner Preference Traits: Trustworthiness, Status and Attractiveness' appeared in *Social Psychology and Personality Science* on Sept 19th, 2017. Wonder why politicians try to get the message across in the first line of their speeches...

What do we know about first impressions then? To start with, that we do change them. This may depend on the person, of course. There are those who will not move an inch from their first impression and those who will. Who is wiser? The second, according to Professor Alex Todorov from Princeton University. In his book *Face Value: The Irresistible Influence of First Impressions* (Princeton University Press, 2017) he states that most first impressions turn out to be wrong!

The reason is quite simple, and, in a way, you know part of it already. It depends on the situation, on society, on the moment... But there are other reasons too. One is that they are based on *superficial factors.* This is the main reason Professor Todorov gives. But I will delve a bit deeper... As we said, body language analysis is "reading behavior" and not "mind reading".

People can behave in a way for different reasons. If we could read these people's minds, we could then be sure about the reason. But as we do not, we can only suppose, suspect them, or even imagine them. We can use deductions to make our assessment to make it rational and reasonable. But it will remain a "very, very high probability" at best, never a "certainty" in scientific terms.

On a personal and professional development level, we need to realize that this applies to body language analysis too. *The professional body language analyst is always ready to change his or her mind and assessment if new evidence, new details come up or simply if a better interpretation is given.* It is a core ethical point of this practice. Basically, we need to be wise, and even wiser than untrained people.

Everybody is different, correct? But when we make quick decisions, like when we have a car accident, we use *"ready-made models and categories* to make our decision." Think about it. At work you are "productive" because you know how to decide quickly. And you do it using simple categories.

With people, these are *stereotypes,* and more often than not, these stereotypes are packed with social and cultural *prejudices.* There are very broad categories we use with stereotypes, for example:

- Trustworthy/untrustworthy
- Likable/not likable
- Strong/weak

- Masculine/feminine
- Extrovert/introvert
- Capable/incapable
- Self-centered/social centered
- Conservative/progressive and traditionalist /innovative
- Rational/irrational
- Old/young.

There are more, but just looking at "masculine and feminine" we realize that defining gender and/or sex is a much more complex matter than finding "the right box". Most people are gender fluid in some way. This does not mean that they necessarily have fluid sexual relationships. People can feel feminine or masculine in different situations. Men can have maternal feelings as women can have paternal ones...

So, an assessment made by quickly fitting a behavior or person into one of these categories is necessarily wrong. At least, let's go back to it and then see if there is more to say, or some shades and hues we need to retouch...

It gets even worse still. Very often, *prejudice sets in.* Linguistic studies in the UK show with no doubt that if you speak Standard English you immediately get the "trustworthy" stereotype but if you speak with a regional accent you get into the opposite box. Skin color is used by many people to people in one or the other category... Age is also a very determinant factor in stereotypes.

We get to the almost comical point in the business world (and white-collar working environment) that the suit color already places you into one or the other stereotype. Black is very self-important and harsh, blue is managerial, brown is old fashioned and maybe trade union sympathizer, green is for those who "want to look different" but no one wearing a green suit will expect to be taken seriously! Really?

So, keeping all this in mind, and always being ready to change our mind on these issues, let's look at a very core of body language and language as a whole: yes or no?

Is It a Yes or a No?

Even in verbal language there are two types of questions and answers:

- Closed questions: where you can only answer yes or no (e.g. "Did you pick up the keys?")
- Open questions: where you can answer in many ways (e.g. "What do you think about Bach's music?").

When reading body language, *understanding yes and no signals is fundamental to direct all the analysis.* They are a bit like the points on a railway. They decide which way the conversation – actually, communication – goes.

Not only this... Imagine this as a cartoon strip... In your mind you have lots of questions which you don't verbalize, but – unbeknown to you – your body is asking them all the time. At the same time, your eyes are fixed on the other person to read her or his answers in her or his body language...

This means that you will need a "set of tools", a broad framework with clear yes and no signals that our bodies give off, more or less consciously.

- *Head nods vs. head shakes* are the clearest, most explicit signs of yes and no. Sometimes, we also do it unconsciously.
- *Open arms vs. folded arms* are again clear signs of yes and no. This gesture can be controlled rationally or at times it happens spontaneously, and this is an interesting distinction to find out when you read body language.
- *Raised eyebrows vs. lowered eyebrows* are a more subtle sign of yes and no. In this case, though it can be done consciously, in most cases these facial expressions are involuntary, spontaneous.
- *Lean towards vs. lean back* can be signs of yes and no. This is not a must though. Leaning forward is usually a positive sign, but leaning back can also be intended as positive, especially when sitting down, as it can mean "I am relaxed".
- *Eye contact vs. no eye contact.* This is possibly the most intriguing way to say yes or no. Do pay attention to movements and changes. A sudden break in eye contact may mean no. But do follow up. If the person comes back into regular eye contact, it may have been a

distraction. If you, on the other hand, notice that after that eye contact is less frequent and "forced or unpleasant", then it most likely is a no.

- *Open vs. locked ankles* often show unconsciously if a person is in agreement or not. It is a yes or no with your feet, which, as we said, we are often unaware of. Because of this, it is one of the most interesting signs for body language analysts. The reason must be clear to you by now: it is unlikely that the person is faking it.

- *Open palms vs. fists.* This often shows openness or resistance. Not literally yes or no, but the fact that the person is receiving what you are communicating or, on the contrary, that the person is resisting it. Maybe it is just a sore topic, though, do not rush to conclusions.

- *Facing vs. turning away* shows that the person is within the conversation or that s/he wants to get away from it. We have seen it and it's another message that you can read in terms of yes and no.

- *Relaxed mouth vs. biting lips* isn't always what it seems. Okay, most times, if someone bites his or her lips it usually means discomfort, so, a no. But sometimes they may do it on purpose to tease you, especially in a romantic situation. So… check the person's eyes and overall body language.

- *Harmonic vs. disharmonic movements.* This may take some practice and experience to note, but it is one of the most consistent yes and no signs. If the listener's body moves to the beat of the speaker's speech, then it's a yes. By movement here we mean *any movement*: eye movement, feet, arms swinging, fingers tapping etc.… This is a clear sign of total accordance and ease. While if the movements are disharmonic, it of course means that the person is not "in tune" with what you are saying… take it as a "no" …

- *Relaxation vs. tension.* It is hard to say no. for some people (like me), it is almost impossible. If you are one of those, learn to say no, for your own sake… Now, moving on… Even people who like to say no (or they think they like it, but here we enter psychology and philosophy…) need to build a barrier between them and you… And that means creating tension. Signs of tension always show a negative attitude.

These are basic pairs of signs that will give you a yes or no reading. But there are some provisos, some "warnings" … As usual…

- *Always read the body as a whole.* We said it and here it's important to remember it. One little negative sign in a series of positive signs does not mean no. It may mean that it's not 100% yes, or that the person was distracted etc. We don't need to be "conspiracy theorists" all the time. However, sometimes conspiracies turn out to be true… So, it might just be that the person pretended to be in agreement but actually wasn't.
- *Observe for a length of time.* You don't want to end up with a first impression, do you? So, keep the observation for as long as possible and base your final assessment on the whole period and behavior. Sometimes it will be easier, sometimes you will have a short time. But *the longer your observation is the more accurate your assessment will be.*

We will come to ideas for giving positive body language signs in a few chapters; don't worry. This is as much a self-development practice as it is a book on reading others. But before we wrap up this chapter, we need to make a final point…

JUDGEMENT VS. ASSESSMENT

Have you noticed that I used the word "assessment" when talking about body language analysis? There is a huge difference between judging and assessing, and this brings the chapter to a nice full circle.

At the beginning of this chapter we talked about how people judge based on first impressions. However, we should never really judge people… But still, the point with judging is that it has consequences. A judge passes a verdict and then if necessary a sentence (guilty, sentenced to community service, for example).

Judging people means that we change our attitudes towards them as a consequence of our evaluations.

Now, let me put you in the shoes of a psychologist, if I may. Psychologists hear all sorts of things. As do doctors, psychiatrists and psychoanalysts etc. But they *do not judge.* They do not put a "value judgement" of "good person vs. bad person" on what they hear. They *assess* instead. What does it mean?

It means that they:

1. *Analyze* (they collect signs, they look at each in detail, then put them together to make sense of them).
2. *Assess* (they draw a conclusion on what they have observed).

An assessment does not need to have consequences. If at all, it is used to help people and to improve situations, like teachers do at school.

We will be taking another dive into the depth of human behavior in a moment. But next, a little summary of all the different types of body language we have.

9

CATEGORIES OF BODY LANGUAGE

Haptics, kinesics, oculesics... You have already learned a lot of technical words concerning body language. These three weird terms, for example, relate to contact, movement and eyes... There is virtually a branch, field or category for each part of the body, and they all have strange names! No, don't worry. I was joking. There isn't one for your little toe and they don't all have names that sound like Greek heroes...

Anyway, this is exactly what we are going to see now. We have seen some, and now it's time to complete the list. We will briefly also go through the ones you have met already, adding some information.

KINESICS

You know that kinesics is the study of body movements within body language. What you don't know yet is that it too is divided into subcategories! All disciplines are like that, they branch out and branch out... It's simply because scholars discover new things all the time and they become more specialized.

And there are three of them, based on the *type of gesture:*

1. *Adaptors:* these are signs that come when the person needs to adjust his

or her balance. They are *"balancing acts"* that often come from either discomfort or excitement. The jump you had when I went "boo!" is an adaptor. So are *many involuntary movements* like sighing, legs shaking, nervous responses like when students click pens in class before a test etc.

2. *Emblems:* these are *very easy to read because their meaning is conventionally agreed upon.* Things like the OK sign, or the thumbs up or thumbs down, high fives, etc.... These have a clear "sign – meaning" code and correspondence, like you find in a dictionary for words.

3. *Illustrators:* these are the signs we use to accompany our speech. You know, those typical gestures each person has when they speak? No person has the same set of illustrators as others. We all use different gestures. On top of this, illustrators in most cases do not have a meaning of their own. But ironically, we soon pick up "the code" the set of meanings of the illustrators of a speaker. Some, however, have positive and some have negative effects.

Kinesics is also used to mean "body language analysis" as a whole. People, however, including scholars, prefer the term "body language" to kinesics in this meaning.

Head Movements

We have seen these, and they include:

1. *Head movements*
2. *Eye movements (oculesics)*
3. *Brow movements*
4. *Mouth and lip movements.*

There is a little trick I want to give you at this stage about facial expressions. You know that the left side of our brain is more rational and the right side more creative. Not "all rational and all creative" as popular belief would have it... Okay. You also know that the brain works in a very strange way. The right eye goes to the left side of the brain, the left nostril goes to the right side of the brain… There's an inversion of sides from the brain and the organs it controls.

Thus, the right side of our face is controlled by the left side of the brain (the more rational one), and the left side of our face is controlled by the right side of our brain (the less rational, more creative and intuitive sign).

Let's apply this to body language. What your left side of the face says is more likely to be spontaneous, not controlled or faked, more in touch with your real emotional state. So, people do wink, a very charming and at times irresistible sign. But the chances are that a right eye wink is "premeditated", and a left eye wink is spontaneous. The chances are – it is never a certainty…

Facial Expressions

There is a difference between facial expression and head (face part) movements. The key note is in "expression". A movement is an easy, factual event to describe: "eyes left" or "head down". But facial *expressions* are indeed a complex system of movements and communication of feelings, even of changes in quality. Think about how you speak with your eyes… *there is much more than movement in the expressive quality of a person*'s eyes. Even of a dog's eyes, to be fair.

What we need to understand is that there are some *general expressive areas.* These are *broad categories of expression* with inner shades and shades between them. Use them as the points of a compass, rather than boxes, when describing facial expressions.

- *Happiness,* which can be expressed with a smile but very often also with your eyes. Try the experiment of covering your mouth in front of a mirror and smiling with your eyes… then try smiling with your mouth and being sad with your eyes. Now you know how to spot a fake smile!
- *Sadness,* which of course is the exact opposite of happiness. It is often revealed by the difficulty of smiling, rather than its absence.
- *Focused,* which is an important state of mind to spot in body language analysis. From the physical and physiological point of view, it is often showed by eyebrows getting closer together. However, the trained

observer will also notice the focus in the speaker's eyes. Focus and determination are also closely connected. If a person looks focused, s/he will also look determined, active, convinced, ready to act etc.

- *Unfocused,* of course, is what you never want to look when you are taking a job interview. However, it is not necessarily negative. There is no "natural value" that says that being unfocused is bad. If you are dreaming, relaxing, imagining, being creative, letting yourself go, being unfocused is very normal indeed! In some cases, it may even show trust. For example, if you are having a romantic time with your partner, being very focused would actually be out of place. Come on, you are not discussing a bank loan!

- *Confident* is the best way to look most times, but even here there may be exceptions, for example, if you are asking for serious help. If you look top confident, you may well get a "no" for answer. A confident person will look centered, full of energy and the facial expression is usually accompanied by an upright and steady body posture. Steady eye contact is also a sign of confidence. Once more, it is a series of signs that gives us the final assessment.

- *Afraid:* people show it in their general body language and facial expression. They will look de-energized, the face will try to "shrink back" and avoid eye contact, of course no signs of happiness and confidence will appear on the face etc. When people become seriously afraid, their first reaction is to protect their face. Covering your face or moving it out of harm's way are typical signs. Notably, the scalp becomes tense when people are afraid, hence the saying "it makes my hair stand on end". This has a technical name too and it is called *"horripilation".*

OCULESICS

Oculesics deserves a section of its own given its importance. Eye reading may even one day become its own discipline, as will "eye speaking".

The problem with oculesics for body language reading is that the reader (a.k.a. you in this case) often has limited access to the person's eyes. You will understand that there is a difference between looking into someone's eyes and "reading them" or standing at a distance and an angle and trying to read someone's eyes.

To train with eye reading, the best exercise is to look for videos. Find videos of people staring at the camera, and not from a distance, there are many politicians you can find, and even salespeople.

Talking about the last ones, forgive me the stereotype. Do you know those classical car sales adverts (furniture too has taken that path)? Look at their eyes... there is something missing, do you notice? They look at the camera, but they are not looking at you. And this is the trick with sales. Salespeople will look at your face, but their stare will stop short of actually looking into your eyes. They will look *at your eyes*, but they will never establish a *full bond, a full contact...*

You understand how delicate this type of reading is? Now, back to the videos... Choose a few and look how far the speakers "pierce the screen" ... What a weird thing that this phrase is no longer used very much... It used to be the "star quality" of actresses and actors...

Then think about your reaction. Which speaker gives you more trust? Which speaker do you feel more "familiar" with? I think we will agree on the answer...

Then there is another issue. We do notice if we are being observed. There is a wonderful book by Dr Rupert Sheldrake out, *The Sense of Being Stared at.* I think I told you already, but do you know that when police people, detectives and secret agents stalk someone they are trained "never to look at their backs". Do you know why? Because the person realizes it.

It's not hearsay, it is mathematical, and all evidence undoubtedly says that we somehow realize when people look at us. We don't know how, and Dr Sheldrake suggests it may be a defense mechanism... Back in the days, when we had to run away from lions, having this ability was an advantage. And zebras and gazelles do have this sense too.

But there is more... Again, all research statistically shows that if a security guard looks at the camera when someone is in front of it the person realizes it. So now they teach security personnel to look at the cameras with the corner of their eyes like they teach detectives to look at people's feet.

So, what's in it for us? That it is hard, in a formal setting and with live readings, to read people's eyes. True. But there is more... and good news...

When you read people's eyes keep your focus as far as possible from the actual eyes of the person you are observing. People realize if you look at their back, let alone if you look into their eyes. It is possibly the most invasive intrusion into someone's privacy before we border into illegality and utter crime...

So, *never look at the person directly into his or her eyes.* Try to keep that angle and look somewhere *in front of his or her eyes.* Note that in many cases you have an advantage: *people who speak know they are being observed... they expect a certain level of eye scrutiny.*

And this leads us to a very important point. This is a famous phenomenon and well researched by linguists...

- When people speak, they look less into other people's eyes than when they listen.
- Conversely, listeners look at the speaker, while the speaker will tend to avoid eye contact.
- However, if listeners fail to look at the person who is speaking, that shows lack of interest, lack of trust, disagreement etc.

... and this is gold dust for body language readers and analysts, both when our observed person is speaking and when s/he is listening... At a board meeting, for example, this may tell you an awful lot about what each person really thinks of what all the others are saying – again though, never jump to conclusions and, especially at board meetings, do factor in the fact that these (and the speakers therewith) are actually most of the time incredibly boring!

HAPTICS

You know haptics by now. The *study of how people touch themselves and touch other people within body language.* You also know that it very much depends on the culture... In Italy men walk round the streets arm in arm (a tradition which I am told is disappearing) but in many other places it would provoke bouts of prejudice galore.

Yet, there is one other factor you will need to take into consideration with haptics: *age.*

Young people tend to touch themselves and each other more. Then, this gets stigmatized as a sign of "childishness" and even "lack of manliness". So, men especially will tend to stop touching others in affectionate ways.

The affectionate touching around adolescence becomes ritualized into a "mock fight" like slaps, "mock slaps", soft punches etc. This is a sign that these young guys actually *need* affectionate touching with their peer...

Anyway, at the same time, women touching themselves becomes "sexualized", by which I don't mean that *they* intend it sexually. I mean that society applies prejudice and sees these as "sexual hints". As a defense mechanism, many young women reduce self-touching (in both frequency and range, for example they avoid certain areas, like legs etc.). But women keep a healthy touching practice with their female peers, unlike men.

Then adulthood sets in and touching is reduced on the whole.

This trend, however, inverts when people are old. Old people usually turn back to touching others and people touch old people with fondness more often than they do adult people. Maybe the "authority challenge" of touching disappears; maybe the "sexual tension" is cleared; maybe people just rediscover their humane nature with old people... who knows?

PROXEMICS

We have seen that proxemics is the *study of how near or far people stand, place themselves and move within body language.* And now we will look at some further information you will find very useful in reading body language...

Have you ever been on an elevator with someone else? How did you feel? No matter who you are, unless you are with someone you are very intimate with (family, close friend or partner) the experience is always the same. People "make themselves small", they look for an empty spot to stare at where they can avoid eye contact, they become rigid and even small talk like "Nice day, isn't it?" becomes a major difficulty...

Why is it so? The fact is that in an elevator you are too close to other people and there is no way this can change. People are "in your space" we say, and this is not just a metaphor. We have an area, like a circle (it's an ellipse on the ground, like an oblong bubble in three dimensions) centered in the middle of our body. This area is called *intimate space.* Any intrusion on this space is a problem.

But if you are in the open, you feel the other person's presence, but you have the option to look away, find comfort on the side. This happens all the time on busy sidewalks. But when you are, for example, talking to someone, not just passing them by, an *intrusion in your intimate space is always felt as very uncomfortable.*

Actually, I lied. We don't have one circle around us: we have four concentric circles (ellipses). *We prefer to have different relationships in the four different spaces, according to how familiar and intimate we are.* And scientists have actually measured these areas. Now, hear they are, and with the radius of the area for each person:

1. *Inner space:* from 0 to 1.5 feet from ourselves. We only allow very intimate people in this space for any length of time.
2. *Personal space:* from 1.5 to 4 feet is the radius of the area where we want normal, everyday (not affectionate) interactions without friends and family. This distance is measured by how far you can stretch your feet comfortably standing. As if we "marked our space" with our feet... like animals do (hold on to this thought; we will return to it soon).
3. *Social space:* from 4 to 12 feet away is where we want to have our everyday social activities with colleagues, people we meet, acquaintances, shop assistants etc. It's the "transactional" area, where we manage our necessary but not friendly relations. Go to your boss's office... Which distance will you keep? You will see that its's within this space.
4. *Public space:* 12 feet or more away from ourselves there is public space,

that space where we allow normal social things to happen freely, without becoming "our business", our concern. Normal activities of course. A man with menacing behavior is better kept a bit further off...

Basically, "our space" has a radius of 12 feet. It's a whole big room...

But here we come to another key principle proxemics:

Territoriality

Did you hold on to that thought? Yes, we are a bit like dogs, wolves, or robins (but not so much cats): we are territorial animals. Not for hunting, but for personal and social relations.

When you are reading someone's body language and proxemics you will need this concept to see, for example:

- If a person allows another person into his or her space easily. You can find out a lot about their relationship from this.
- If a person keeps other people out of their space and who they keep out. You can see his "hierarchy" of friends or even actual hierarchies. Presidents, kings, queens and rock stars keep others they don't regard their peer at a distance, in the public space... It can be a power game.
- If someone tries to intrude into someone else's space. This can be quite annoying, and it may mean that the person is trying to gain something. This "something" though may depend. In some cases, it even feels "slimy", in a working setting it may give away the careerist, but it might just be a request for friendship in other situations...

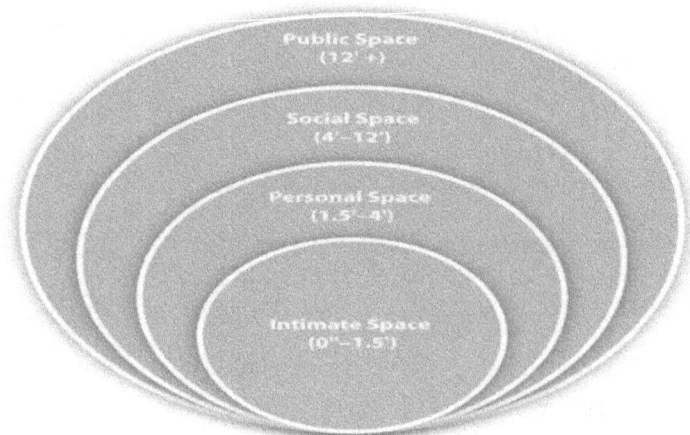

Territoriality again works on a cline, on a continuous line from "almost not territorial" to "very territorial" and it depends on three main factors:

- The relationship between the people involved (close or distant)
- The situation (informal, formal; private, public)
- The individuals (some people are more territorial than others).

When reading body language, you want to try to distinguish these three. For example, if the first two are set (a meeting between two businesspeople) and you see one of them being very territorial, then you know that this person is or is trying to be authoritative and dominant.

In fact, there is a direct link between being territorial and being dominant, being the alpha dog (I prefer it to alpha male...) or trying to exert authority.

POSTURE

Posture is not technically a movement nor is it given by a single part of your body. Thus, we can see it as its own category within body language.

Posture is very important when training to read body language for many reasons:

- It is most often the *first thing we notice at a distance.* So, it is key to the notorious *first impressions* we talked about before.
- Most times, *we read the messages of posture subconsciously* and only sporadically consciously. This tells us that posture speaks directly to our subconscious.
- *Reading posture trains you to read the body as a whole.*

However, having said this, there is one part of the body which is very key to posture and it is in the middle of our body: our *chest*.

The chest

The chest is key to posture as it is the "central part of our body". What we can say about the chest is whether it is:

- *Centered or off center.* If the chest is centered, so, not off to the left or right, it projects confidence and authority, on the other hand, when off center it may also indicate relaxation, friendliness, informality, intimacy etc.
- *Leaning forward, leaning backward or straight.* This shows attitudes towards what is being said. Forward means agreement, empathy, interest. Backward may mean diffidence, even worry, or repulsion. At times, it only means relaxation as we said, especially if sitting down. A straight posture means "I am in control", or even "I am fine with myself". Noble people (look at the Queen again) are taught to keep a very upright chest all the time to project authority and status.
- *Stretching or shrinking.* We can stretch our chest out or "make it small", and of course, it means "stability" or "nerves and uncertainty" accordingly.

We had not talked about the chest so far, but as you can see, it too matters.

The neck and head

The neck too is important for posture. Forward, down, backward, sideways etc. positions give different signals. Let's see them.

- *Forward neck and head* mean interest and involvement.
- *Backward neck and head* mean distance and even self-protection.
- *Head tilted*, as we said, indicates deep thought, even creativity.
- *Head down* as we said is most often a negative sign, showing tiredness or shame or uncertainty, or in any case an unwillingness to engage.

Legs and feet

The way we keep our legs and feet are too part of our posture. We will look at sitting positions later on, but for now we shall focus on standing positions.

- *Legs partly apart (one foot) and feet straight or outward,* the singer's position, as we called it, is a sign of *confidence, self-awareness and balance.*
- *Legs close together and feet too:* this can be a sign of worry or even insecurity or perceived threat.
- *Legs and feet spread out* (like resting on a step, sideways etc.) is a sign of great ease, confidence, a sense of security, informality and also self-confidence.

We already talked about how arms are used to "appropriate the space", thus they have a very important role in hierarchical relations, but now let's look at sitting postures.

Sitting postures

How people sit is telling. Now, once upon a time, teachers actually taught *how to sit.* Then of course, most students never learned it. But in high society in the UK and Europe in general, sitting "properly" is a clear sign of "good upbringing" ...

But more than a sign that you went to an expensive school, it is also a way to project authority. Look again at the Queen and her mother. Examine how they sit. That is "sitting properly" and what does it translate into? Imperturbability.

They form perfect 90-degree angles with their legs and their abdomen. They look like geometrical figures if you look at them. The Queen Mother was noted by body language analysts for her perfect posture well into her old age, when she was in severe physical decline and needed to use a crutch... Still sitting perfectly upright.

The legs should be parallel but a small distance apart (a few inches) and they should form perfect vertical lines, no diagonals allowed...

This is the same posture you will find is used to depict pharos, kings, queens, popes, emperors and cardinals throughout history. Why? You know the answer: it projects authority.

Any deviation from this may tell the observer quite a few things, for example:

- *Feet back, with calves retracted under the body, or legs bending backward.* This is a sign of "self-protection". The person is not fully confident with what is happening. There may be some nervousness and even anxiety. If to this, you add...
- *Crossed ankles,* which always means a closure, then the sign is that the person wants to disengage. S/he does not seem at ease at all and is trying to "get out of it" most probably. This "it" may just be a difficult question, not necessarily the whole situation.
- *Leaning forward and backward,* as we have already said, mean "engaging" and "not engaging" or "relaxing".
- *Parts of the body off symmetry,* like chest off center and leaning, legs over the armrest, resting on one elbow etc.... These are signs of informality, of a friendly attitude, of relaxation and "feeling at home", but they may also appear rude in some situations, especially in formal settings and with people that you don't know well.

There are also cultural influences. In the USA, people are on average more relaxed with posture than they are in many other countries, including Europe and Asian countries. You will never see a Japanese CEO with his feet on the table... he may even get fired for it.

HOW YOU SAY IT MATTERS

We said that body language analysis is not language analysis (that's another science) but there are obviously overlapping zones. And we said that all those "mm's" and "er's" are in this overlapping zone... As are accent, intonation etc. Now we shall see exactly what these categories tell us in terms of body language analysis.

And yes, you guessed it, there are categories and subcategories here too!

Paralanguage

This is what we say but is not verbal. So, all those grunts, mm's and er's. These are fairly easy to understand in most cases, but we just need to remember that we do need to take note of these.

But there is more, and we are getting to it straight away...

Vocalics

Vocalics is the *study of the vocal quality* of speakers. And this is huge, actually. Let me tell you a few facts...

Not everybody has the same range, both in pitch and expressiveness (actual quality of the voice), but we all have more than one *register* or *voice.* Let's hear your "child voice"! You see, you too have different voices. Now, give me your "scolding voice" ... You got the point.

Thing is, some people have a large repertoire of voices. Imitators for example, but also many actors and other people. You can actually train to get new voices...

And then there is the actual range: some people can go up and down the scales like singers... This is what we call:

Pitch

Exactly the same as with singing, and exactly the same with singers. Some singers have many notes, others have fewer... So do people. Some men can get their voices to reach the soprano, range also when speaking, others, on the other hand, always sound like a bass or baritone.

We use exactly the same categories as for opera singers. In the end, when we speak, we use notes too. And pitch is very telling...

- If a person has a *flat pitch*, this may indicate boredom, disinterest, tiredness, or even (hear, hear!) depression. Yes, one of the first signs of depression a psychology notes is a flat, monotonous pitch.
- A *low pitch throughout* tends to project authority, severity and seriousness.
- A *higher than usual pitch* may indicate the opposite, so things like

playfulness, empathy and informality or even vulnerability, but sometimes it is used to mock the other person (we will see that in the "tone" section).

- *A varied pitch* will usually carry the meaning properly and, unless exaggerated, it will project competence and interest at the same time. That's the pitch of a good teacher or public speaker in general.
- *An exaggerated pitch* may tell you that the person is not fully in control, maybe simply due to excitement.

But the most important thing is that the person *adapts the pitch to the circumstance.* You don't use the same pitch playing with a child or speaking at a board meeting or at a drunken birthday party and at a funeral, I hope!

Tone

The tone of the voice is one of those things that is not mathematically measurable, like many things in music, for example "andante con brio". And that is tone when we speak. But we all understand it. There are so many key tones, and areas in between, so, again, use them as the points of a compass rather than rigid boxes.

- *Factual*
- *Serious*
- *Playful*
- *Annoyed*
- *Enthusiastic*
- *Warm*
- *Cold*
- *Cynical, sarcastic, ironic*
- *Doubtful*
- *Threatening.*

These are things you need to take into consideration, a bit like the subtitles to films... They are not actually fully part of the film, but they help us understand it...

Functions of vocalics

These are functions of communication. Let me explain... Function is a term that comes from grammar and it means "why do we use this form". For example, a verb has a function, which is to express an action or a state. Similarly, a past tense has a function, which is to talk about something that happened in the past etc.

But when we talk, we help each other out, we contradict each other, we interact all the time. So, we need to see how we do it, and *with which functions.* And these are the main ones:

- *Accenting* is emphatic, it serves to underline, stress and even agree or make a point.
- *Regulating,* which means that when we speak we give signals to the other person about turn taking or waiting. These are signs about the conversation itself, a bit like road signs... But they tell us the intentions of the speaker. Lowering the voice or slowing down at the end of your turn (followed by eye contact). Or raising your voice to say "I am still talking" etc.
- *Contradicting,* this is when you use your intonation to say, "I mean the opposite". It means "contradicting the verbal message, the words you are using" not the other person.
- *Substituting* is when you use nonverbal sounds to replace words (like the famous "er" to mean "hold on I need to think").
- *Complementing,* which is whenever you add meaning to a word (any meaning) using your voice. This is the most general term. For example, you can say "I would love to go to Paris" with "love" pronounced "loooave", then you are expressing a yearning, strong desire. So, you are complementing the word itself (not contradicting it but adding to it).

CHRONEMICS

Timing is also important, and chronemics (another Greek sounding word) is how we use timing when speaking. Of course, this too is part of both language analysis and body language analysis.

Going fast or slow, speeding up or slowing down, taking pauses are all important elements of speech and body language.

The general idea is that:

- *If you go slow you are confident and in control.*
- *If you go fast you show lack of confidence, interests or a tine that you are trying to "get it out" rather than "get it understood".*
- *If you slow down, you mark something which is important.*
- *If you speed up it may mean that you are not too interested in it or you want to get over it, leave etc.* (or maybe the bell is about to ring).

Then *pauses* are important:

- *Regular short pauses show confidence and competence.*
- *No pause at all or short and infrequent pauses show the opposite, lack of confidence.*
- *Long pauses show drama, importance and a sense of great control.*

And this last point leads us to an important observation. *You should read all these in conjunction with body language signs.*

For example, let's take the long pause. It's a very difficult thing to achieve. Holding attention when being silent is a thing only phenomenal actors and actresses can do for more than very few seconds.

But if during the pause the speaker looks calm, has a confident posture and may even look around, then that shows the speaker has the audience literally charmed...

If during the pause you start fumbling with what you have in your pockets, if you look down at your papers etc.... I bet the audience will be left with a totally different impression...

And this leads us straight into the next chapter... Sometimes yes means no and no means yes even with words. But let me ask you a question: is it the same with body language?

POSITIVE VS. NEGATIVE

Good vs. evil, love vs. hate, light vs. darkness are all archetypes of how we think and how we see the world. One needs the other to define itself and yet it is the opposite. The story of thought on positive vs. negative goes back to early Greek philosophers for sure (Epicurus, e.g.) in the West while the East has a whole school of thought based on it, represented by the Tao, that symbol of opposites that has amazed generations.

Grand starting paragraph, but what does it mean in practical terms and body language? Sure, we have already touched on this topic a few times in this book. That's natural because it is very basic but also far reaching and all-permeating. But now it is time to explore it fully. What is more, this chapter will be useful for two areas of your body language studies:

- How to read positive and negative body language.
- How to keep a positive body language.

Now in fact you have learned quite a lot about reading body language and only a few things about controlling your own body language. In the coming chapters we will turn more closely towards the second...

But without further ado, let's get into the thick of it straight away!

HOW TO TELL POSITIVE VS. NEGATIVE BODY LANGUAGE

There are *two main ways of saying if body language is positive or negative: the body language itself and contradictions.* Let's see them.

The body language itself

There are *body language signs that are clearly, solely, or primarily negative or positive.* The head shake for "no" is maybe the clearest and most recognized. But even saying no with your fingers is common. Or putting your hands forward showing your palms.

These are either *emblems* and *adaptors* and even something in between, like the palms forward gesture. These are usually easy to tell. But remember that the "ay or nay" meaning is only *at face value.*

What do we mean by this? That we need to remember that we often say the opposite of what we mean. It's the literal (and literary, but linguistic too) meaning of *irony: saying one thing but meaning another.* And we do it with our body language too! Like the mother shaking her head but smiling we saw a few chapters ago...

Yet, the key point to take home here is that *we can only use irony with voluntary body language.* So, when reading body language, you really need to pay a lot of attention to which signs are voluntary (and the meaning can be willfully changed) and involuntary ones (adaptors for example, but also as you know eye movements, breathing etc.).

To understand if a sign has had its meaning changed, however, we need to use the second method:

Contradictions

Whenever there is a contradiction, one of the two terms must be positive and the other negative. There's no escaping this... What we need to determine then is only which sign is positive and which is negative... That looks straightforward in theory, but in practice it is not that easy... Why? First of all, *where can you find contradictions?* The problem is not that it will be hard for you to find them... It's that there are too many in most cases!

You will, in fact, need to look at contradiction between all "communicative means" and "factors"... Let me explain:

- *Contradictions in body language signs within one person.*
- *Contradictions in body language signs between the participants* (the observed person and the others s/he is interacting with).
- *Contradictions between body language and what people say verbally.*
- *Contradictions between what people say and how they say it.*
- *Contradictions between the body language and the topic itself* (talking about children with a sneer can show a contradiction between a topic we should find pleasant and positive and the body language...)
- *Contradictions between body language and the context as a whole* (informal body language in a formal situation... Just imagine a soldier who picks his nose, or just yawns while receiving a medal... It's a stupid image, I know but it does show you how far we can go from what the situation expects of us).

Thus, you will need to find where a sign clashes with another sign and look everywhere for it. But then your task is to find out which of the two signs, positive or negative, represents the position (meant as mind, idea, opinion or feeling) of the person you are analyzing...

But to learn this, you will have to wait till the next Chapter!

Now let's turn to ourselves, let's apply what we know about positive and negative signs to ourselves.

HOW OFTEN DO YOU SHOW POSITIVE AND NEGATIVE BODY LANGUAGE?

We are far less aware of ourselves than we usually believe. Most people are convinced they know exactly what they look like, how they are appearing to others... If only they could see themselves on camera! Did I tell you about slouching? Do you know that I was not aware of it until an opera singing teacher told me? I was an adult by then already... This means that I spent about 30 years or so not knowing about my own negative body language...

Look around you, take a walk in the streets... Look at how many people give off negative body language and how many people give off positive body language...

Actually, let's try a little experiment... Go to a busy road near where you live and check positive and negative body language at rush hour on a weekday. Then go back there at the weekend and do the same...

Most probably, you will find that the rush hour walk gave you an overwhelming prevalence of negative body language and the weekend one gave you more positives...

NEGATIVE BODY LANGUAGE

There are many factors that make us give positive or negative body language (and this is a matter of "prevalence" not total exclusion of positives or negatives):

- *Personal health* (the most obvious explanation in many cases)
- *State of mind*
- *Context* (pleasant vs. unpleasant, stressful or relaxing...)
- *Activity* (a leisurely stroll in the park vs. being late for work)
- *Even the weather will bring out positive or negative body language...*

These are factors I am asking you to note down for the next Chapter, which is strictly connected with this one... For now, however, this should prove one thing, namely:

- If of all these factors, your intention is only part (and not even the whole) of one point, "state of mind", most of the positive and negative body language signs are determined by factors independent of our will!

But there is another corollary to this, another conclusion we can draw: *if you display negative body language, don't feel guilty about it.* It is not "your fault"; the context, repeated activities etc. literally train our body to give off negative body language signs. Slouching being maybe the most exemplary once more...

A slouch is usually developed over years. Day in day out, you use a negative posture until it "feels natural and neutral" to you and you don't even realize that you are doing it. Instead, it will always appear as negative to people who see you...

Imagine now you are starting an acting course... We'll start with "wiping the slate" or "clearing the space" ... Before we start correcting our body language, we need to eliminate negative body language... And in order to eliminate negative body language we need to become aware of it.

Now, take the time you need. But this time I will ask you to get a small notebook and a pencil and keep them with you all the time. For a week or any time you need. In this notebook, I am asking you to *note down all your negative body language habits.* To find them out you can:

- Record yourself, or ask a friend to record you, especially at a time when you are not aware of it.
- Look at yourself in mirrors and shop windows when you walk in the street. Try to "catch yourself unaware" ... I mean, whenever you see a mirror, just look at yourself as if by surprise, without correcting your posture etc.... I did it, and I still do it a lot... This is really handy also when you are correcting your body language.
- Every now and then, stop; shift your focus from whatever you are doing to your body, and scan it for negative body language signs (especially posture with this exercise). Don't do this when you are driving though!
- Ask friends or family members. Do tell them to be honest. Sit down and explain, "You need to be a real friend. Honestly, tell me the truth..." then ask about posture, facial expressions etc.... go through the whole list and note down things that may be negative. Here, then use your discretion. Your friend may well also tell you things that get on his or her nerves for personal reasons, but they are not necessarily negative body language.

After you know which signs you need to eliminate from your body language, we can move to the next phase... eliminating them.

Eliminating Negative Body Language

As you may guess, this can take some time. So, the sooner you start, the better.

First of all, *start with the most prominent one.* In particular start with *posture.* You know by now that it is the most noticeable body language sign. And your best friend here is a *mirror:*

- Every day when you wake up check yourself in the mirror and take a correct, open and upright posture.
- Set yourself reminders to check on your posture during the day (use that ringtone).
- When you get home at night, again, go to the mirror and correct your posture.
- Doing some stretching and physical exercise can help a lot with correcting your posture.

You should notice that *once you correct your posture, many other negative signs should disappear.* In fact, lots of them are consequences of it, including your gait, the way you look at people (straight, from below or from above...), how open your gestures are etc.

Then, pick on a sign in turn, choosing the big ones, or the ones you dislike most. One by one spend a few days correcting it with a similar method, till you feel confident that you can move to the next one.

Once you have "leveled" the first few major body language negatives you habitually display, it is time to move to the next phase, *introducing and displaying positive body language.*

POSITIVE BODY LANGUAGE

To start with, developing and building positive body language does not mean being "dishonest". In most cases, it means *aligning your body language with your actual personality.* Most of us *are* positive people, but we just don't look it.

Yet again, *start with your posture!* If you have followed the exercises so far, you have already started correcting your posture. But there is more to correcting than just eliminating negatives...

Shall we look at two concepts that people often confuse, to make this point clear? "Confidence" and "being bossy". Once you have eliminated the "non-confident" signs (like slouching, making yourself small, avoiding frontal positions etc.) you can build a new "image" of yourself. Unfortunately, especially in the business world, the idea of "bossy" has become a replacement for "confident".

You can even see this in a general shift among politicians... They used to stand and look confident, in control, authoritative *but not aggressive.* Instead, among many politicians nowadays the attitude you see is that of the bully (which as you know is all but confident in reality). Lots of "chest out ready to fight" and fists and closure to the audience...

You need to choose which image of yourself you wish to project. It is literally like building a character for an actor or actress... You see, good actresses and actors "level their real personality off" and add all the traits of the character they need to embody, perform and bring to life.

Study how actors and actresses change their gait, posture and even facial expressions with each new character. I am talking about professionals here.

But this leads us into another trick... Choose a person you admire. This could be a famous person or a friend or family member... *Study that person's body language:*

- How would you describe it in a few words?
- What is/are the key trait(s) of his or her body language? Choose a handful.
- Can you try to imitate them?

Imitation is a very profound learning method... We learn to speak by imitating our parents. What I am asking you to do is to choose a *body language role model* and *introduce some traits of his or her body language in yours.* Not all – we are not in the cloning business here.

Also do keep in mind that what may look good on a person may not on another. So, be self-critical and be ready to change in case...

For facial expression, the really best exercise is to *pull faces in the mirror.* Even facial expressions are habitual, and we reduce the range of expressions when we are stressed, we have a monotonous life, we are always being judged (including at work or school!)

The fact is that a person with a wide and free range of facial expressions will go far... And as usual, I don't just mean business, but also personal relationships. Pulling faces is like "stretching for your face". It exercises the muscles we then use (often unconsciously) to produce facial expressions.

Bold and expressive facial expressions become simpler and better marked if you train and build the very muscles that produce them. This at the same time has a "backdoor effect", which means that you will at the same time become more confident. Expressing yourself with confidence literally builds your inner strength.

Then choose a few major body language signs you wish to introduce and work on one at a time... Again, the mirror is your best friend here. Play little scenes in front of it, and if you do it regularly, you will *internalize this gesture.* So, when it comes in handy in a normal, everyday situation, it will come out naturally.

A few signs are enough to change the overall perspective that people have on you, and in any case how you project your personality...

Positive and Negative, True and False

Coming to a conclusion, you now know how to tell positive and negative apart but also how to build a more positive body language for yourself. And this is closely linked with what is coming up next: a whole chapter to develop your skills in telling lies and appearing truthful.

11

LIAR, LIAR, PANTS ON FIRE!

Pants are actually *not* a reliable way of finding out if someone is lying to you... Trust me, there are much better ways, and you know some already. Most importantly, we said that lies are not detected by a single body language sign (like touching your nose, that's a myth) but by reading many signs in context and matching them against the words spoken.

The true/false dimension of our communication (both verbal and non-verbal) is so big and complex that we need a whole chapter to explore it. And this is exactly it!

WHY DO WE LIE? IS IT ALWAYS INTENTIONAL?

Most of us have lied at some stage in our lives. Most of us will do it again. Lying is regarded as "unethical", "wrong", "disgusting" and even "a sin" in religious terms, but it is so widespread and common that, behind this public condemnation, *most societies, especially Western ones, actually condone lying (to a certain extent) behind the scenes.*

Currently lying is even being promoted. Only a few years ago, a politician caught lying even on a minor issue would be forced to resign. Nowadays politicians lie openly, and some people even esteem them for this; the idea that all that matters is "getting to the top" and "outsmarting others" has really had major negative effects on our moral compass.

So, why do we lie? There isn't a specific reason, but we can start with a facilitating factor (rather than motive): *it is implicitly condoned by society and it is becoming even more so.* But while this may give the "all clear" to lie to some people, it does not tell us why they decide to lie in the first place...

And the reasons are many... To start with, *when is lying actually lying?* I've not lost my mind... Let me give you an example:

- Is a child telling a story lying?
- Is a writer writing a fiction novel lying?
- Is a teacher giving a simplified explanation to make it accessible lying?
- Is recalling "creatively" filling in the gaps of your memory with "what you think happened" lying?

On the first one, I think we can agree... But this habit can keep going till you are an adult, and some people may then end up *literally not being sure about what is true and what is not.* For these people telling a lie is like saying the truth. These are *pathological liars.* Of course, they are not (that) many and they suffer from a very serious mental condition.

But people can convince themselves that what they are saying is true every now and then... It happens, either because you don't remember well, or because we actually do sometimes lie to ourselves...

It happens very often when people's life compass, their very basic beliefs, their ideology etc. are challenged. Imagine the famous Bishop who refused to look into Galileo's telescope. You see, for him the choice was: change all you have ever believed in or lie to yourself this once. It's not a conscious choice though... it's subconscious. And most of us do it quite often.

This leads to *cognitive bias,* which means that there is a difference between what you subconsciously know is true and what you consciously say is true. Most *prejudice can be read as cognitive bias.*

Even in this case, most people are not even aware of lying, because they are lying to themselves.

But there are many more reasons why people lie, even much more practical ones:

We lie to fend off interest, for example. If some stranger asks you, "How much have you got in your wallet?" You are most likely going to reply with a lie, especially if you happen to have a big sum. Why? You are *"giving a red signal" to the other person*; you are saying, "This is none of your business".

This is very common in stores and shops. Many people reply with a lie to an insistent shopkeeper or shop assistant. "Come on, buy these socks, they are on sale and high quality!" What would you say? "Stop bothering me you fool!" or a more innocent (but false), "No thanks, I have them already!" A creative and cheeky liar may say, "I never wear socks, thank you!"

In these situations, the lie is detected. You don't even expect the shop assistant to believe you, do you? You just want to give them a cul-de-sac in the conversation, an "access denied" sign...

We lie to help people, and these are white lies. Most people think that white lies are the only acceptable ones. But "acceptable" is a sociocultural value, and I would say that society accepts the previous type of lies too.

We lie because we are afraid. This is a habit we pick up at school or as children anyway. We are afraid of the consequences of telling the truth, and so we lie. "Did you eat the slice of cake I left for your sister, Charlie?" and of course the answer is "No, a mouse came and took it away!"

This just becomes more sophisticated, better honed, more "professional" but for many of us it remains a *survival technique* well into our adult and especially professional life. The fact that in many places your workplace is a very competitive environment, such lies become very common.

Not just this, but because we often see that *those who lie have fast-tracked careers in many places, lying itself even becomes an advantage!* People lie to make money. Quite simply...

Here we certainly reach the opposite of those who lie compulsively. People who lie out of selfishness do it fully consciously – at first! Like all habits, it then can become *internalized and naturalized and therefore become subconscious.* And then you become a compulsive liar. It's a circle.

But there is more… How about our last case, the "filling in the blanks" with a bit of imagination? Is it lying?

It certainly is if you are giving a witness statement in court. But this is a legacy of our childhood experience, when telling stories (imaginative ones) is part not only of growing up, but of finding your place in society.

Think back to your early years at school, at elementary, or primary school… Do you remember that friend who always had amazing stories that now sound like fairy tales? Do you also remember how popular s/he was?

There are people who keep this liking for "coloring" their stories into their adulthood, a bit like comedians do when they tell a joke… Again, how far is this acceptable? It's hard to put a general rule on this…

Importantly, there are also clinical problems. People with any form of *dementia* may use this very method of *"filling in the gaps"* to make sense of what they are recalling and saying. If you know anyone with dementia you will have noticed it. They say something true then insert something that's completely false. This is of course acceptable.

But it leads us to another case: *people lie because their memory is wrong.* With irrelevant episodes but also with painful ones, time plays a little trick… Over years, it starts changing our memory. In most cases, we tend to remember things in a "better version" of the reality. This is a self-defense mechanism with painful memories… Sometimes, however, the opposite is true.

A very curious phenomenon is that people often remember being on the right side of an argument while actually they were on the wrong side at the time… A sort of "I told you so" in retrospect…

And then there are cases when *people lie without actually knowing why.* The lie just comes out of their mouth, often when answering in a hurry or under pressure. They realize that – well, it's as if someone inside of them has beaten them to the answer and told a lie... And what can they do? In most cases they are taken aback, realize they lied and pretend nothing has happened. More rarely, people correct themselves.

Then of course, you have those who lie to you out of evil intentions, like getting information out of you, getting money out of you, stealing your ideas etc. And these of course, are the main ones we need to look out for.

So, no, lying is in many cases totally subconscious. In some cases, people think they are telling the truth (but is it lying), in other cases people lie but they are not aware that it is wrong, and there are then those who lie because they just want to...

7 WAYS TO SPOT A LIAR

As usual, we need some theory to see the big picture, but we also want some practical tips. However, before we move forward, at the risk of sounding repetitive... we are going to see 7 signs that can *make you suspect that someone is lying*. But importantly, *none of these on its own will tell you that the person is lying.*

Be professional, look out for these signs but then *always look at body language as a whole, collect as many signs as possible and base your assessment on the whole, not the individual sign and finally check the signs against the actual words of the person.*

1. *Lack of eye contact;* this is by far one of the best ways of finding out if someone is telling the truth or lying. But beware! Some people may actually be shy! Or maybe they don't trust you?
2. *Sudden change of head position;* this may signal a sudden change of thought. Matched against what the person is saying, it can reveal a contradiction. This sign is especially useful in readings, lectures, presentations etc.
3. *Rigidity;* a very stiff, nervous and static posture may indicate lying. Lying in general makes us tense, and that means physically as well. Lie detectors in fact monitor muscles as well... But remember to read

everything in context... If we took this rule as absolute, we would conclude that our old acquaintance the Queen has never uttered an honest word in her life!

4. *Covering your mouth;* this is an instinctive reaction when you realize that you said something wrong, and it may come out when someone is lying. But again, beware, *it does not only come out when you are lying.* It can also express uncertainty, even concern, or a closure to the speaker.

5. *Tense lips;* tense lips usually show, you guessed it, uneasiness with the words you say. And the most detectable sign of this is when *people curl their lips.* Once more, it may also mean that it's a difficult thing to say, not necessarily a lie.

6. *Sudden change of breathing;* breathing is often involuntary, and if you become suddenly nervous, anxious etc. you will need more oxygen to calm yourself down, and your breathing accelerates automatically. This however, needs to be quite sudden or it is more likely to be due to other reasons. What is more, breathing can change pace due to other factors: general anxiety, stress, heat, dehydration etc.

7. *Frequent jitters;* this seems quite non-specific, but actually it is. All sudden changes of behavior, movements, little twitches and signs of nervousness are clear signs of worry, and they may be signs of lying.

You see, the point is that we usually feel at ease with the truth and the average person worries when lying. But there are pathological liars who lie "with a straight face" as we say informally. Luckily pathological liars are comparatively rare, and even they give off signs to expert observers. Politicians, for example, may avoid facing the audience with their breast, and turn it sideways... That could indicate awareness of lying.

In fact, as a bonus sign...

Covering vulnerable parts; the politician hiding his or her chest is trying to protect a vulnerable part (his or her heart and other vital organs). Similarly, people cover their neck, sometimes eyes, belly etc. when they feel threatened. Lying and being caught is a threat, isn't it?

Yes, because you will be judged etc. So, the expectation of being judged and caught makes you protect a vulnerable part.

IDENTIFY THE KIND OF LIAR YOU ARE FACING

We have seen that there are many reasons for lying. Surprise, surprise, there are also different types of liars. The categories of liars (taxonomy of liars, if you want to impress your friends with a technical term) partly depend on the reason for lying but they are also determined by behavioral patterns when lying.

These may include factors like how often they lie, how easily they lie etc.... All in all, we can group them into 6 categories.

1. *Compulsive liars;* these are the hardcore liars, people who lie consistently and with an attitude like they don't even care if you find out that they are lying. For many of them, the important thing is that you listen to their lies. Some politicians are like this and many conmen: on a large audience, they know that someone will believe them. They don't care at all if the others find them out.

Having said this, *compulsive liars are easy to spot. They display a wide range of body language signs that suggest lying.* They will avoid eye contact; they tend to turn away from the people they are talking to etc.

What is more, they are also easy to find through what they say: their stories don't add up and often become implausible. Actually, the more people give them positive feedback, the more they exaggerate their lies.

There are two types of compulsive liars, *narcissistic liars* and *habitual liars.*

> *a. Narcissistic liars* do it because they want attention. These are usually story tellers and they add and embellish their stories with false details. They basically are like those children who are so popular with peers because they "tell tales" – only they are adults and they should know better.
>
> *b. Habitual liars* are simply people who will lie all the time out of habit. We change and we can learn any bad habit if we "train" (even unwillingly) long enough. And these are people who have been brought

up lying all the time and just find it natural to, like for a dancer it is natural to do the splits and not for us... With habitual liars it is very difficult to trace the reason why they are lying. In fact, in many cases there is none...

2. Pathological liars are not compulsive liars because they don't do it all the time out of habit or attention seeking. They *respond to stimuli by lying.* They lie constantly, but not indiscriminately.

Of all liars, *pathological liars are the most difficult to find out.* This is because they have become so accustomed to lying that they display very few signs. These are the ones who "lie in with a straight face". They often keep lying undetected for long periods of time, and they will use this to their advantage.

In fact, they will often have good careers in competitive environments. You can surely guess how... by lying to your boss and lying to you... And by keeping that straight face that hides all their lies for years...

There is a beautiful technical word for this *pseudologia fantasica* (Latin for "fanciful false thinking" or "fanciful false argument") ...

3. Sociopathic liars; these are dangerous! They too tend to be pathological liars. However, they are classed as sociopathic liars because they fall within a much more serious mental condition: sociopathy (psychopathy is similar), which means that they have *no ability to feel empathy.* What does it mean? That they do not understand other people's feelings at all. These can literally watch a person being tortured and they feel *nothing at all* in grave cases.

Sociopaths and psychopaths also lie a lot. They do it because they only see people as "objects", or "things to exploit" and they are incapable of thinking about other people's good. They do it to profit themselves.

Unfortunately, they will feel nothing when lying apart from risks for themselves. Let me explain... They do not become tense because of the very fact that they are lying, and they are uncomfortable with it. They don't care about it. For them you could even die there and then. They are only afraid that you may catch them.

This means that they may not have all the signs of big liars, despite being super big liars themselves. But they may display more "protect vulnerable parts" signs, like turning sideways etc.

But there is a trick to find out of you are dealing with a sociopath or psychopath... *Check their reaction to emotions. If they have none, that's a very clear indicator.* Look at reactions to emotional stimuli... They will either fake concern (and they are bad at that because they don't understand it), or even cut it short and show uneasiness with "being put in the spot".

And if there are no signs? Throw a little trap! Tell them you are very uncomfortable with something they are saying and observe them. You will get no body language sign of real emotional involvement... And remember, these people are seriously dangerous. It's no hyperbole. They will ruin anybody's life with no remorse.

4. *Careless liars;* this is another bad category of liars. They are often the cause of broken relationships... I hope you have never had a story with one of them in your life, but if you have, I am sure you already understand what sort of person we are talking about.

These people will lie, in fact, carelessly, as if it did not matter at all. They often even have moral values in life, but when they need to lie, they suddenly feel nothing about them. These are the typical people who will lie to you about extramarital relationships for example. Or those that may lie to you about where they have been etc.

Despite lying carelessly, they do display signs. For example, they will become nervous (fidgety, closed posture, even raise their voice) and even restless or aggressive as soon as you probe their lies. You see, they lie to you and they think they got away with it and you should just believe them. They don't expect you not to trust them!

5. *Occasional liars;* these are *usually bad liars,* but they are also very common. We all occasionally lie. The fact is that *they repent about lying most times and very quickly.* Actually, it is virtually impossible that an occasional liar will not have second thoughts and moral issues about his or her lie, even if small.

They are very easy to spot because they will display generously that they have lied with their body language. But what is more, just like with fibbing children, after lying both their body language and behavior will usually change.

6. White liars; I wanted to close on a positive note. White lies are good lies. And white liars do it for your own good, so, maybe together with some lying signs, you will also see signs of *empathy and even protection,* like a warm look, palms towards you, etc.…

Good white liars, if you want to become one, also have a steady, comforting but "refracting" eye contact. I'll explain, they know in their heart that they are doing it for you, so they will look into your eyes and they will express love and care, but at the same time, they will invite you not to probe too far. Just repeating to yourself "I am doing it for you" when looking into the person's eyes will have an effect.

However, this effect may end up being that the person understands you are lying, but that you are doing it for her or his sake... You can't lie with your eyes...

THOSE WHO LIE BEHIND THE SAFETY OF A SCREEN

The issue of fake news and disinformation could not be more topical. It may well be one of the biggest problems that the democratic world is facing right now. We are not here to make a full list of reliable and unreliable sources, though I suppose you already have your own favorites and least favorites.

But this topic partly merges with our field... To start with, *you cannot analyze the body language to someone who is writing an email or a Facebook post.* Or even a newspaper article to be correct! That is a disadvantage.

What is more, as the title suggests, *lying behind a screen is easier. People just feel safer doing it.* You may wonder why...

- The person they are lying to is not present in person.
- They can double check what they write, while if you lie face to face you just get one chance...

- People often read these posts and messages very quickly.
- The platform itself (social media etc.) gives the, credibility… the "I read it on Facebook" syndrome…
- With modern technology, that can prepare fake evidence (photoshopped images or even links to other lying sources).

So, what can we do about it? I will answer this with another question: are these people totally exempt from that "lying shame" that appears in body language?

The answer is that in most cases they are not. You see, they feel protected, but they still feel a level of uneasiness!

And this will then translate into behavior. Okay, it's not body language but it is related, contiguous in a way… And here are a few things you can look out for:

- *How credible is the account itself?* An account is not a person, but many of the fake news spreaders also use fake accounts. Some are easy to spot. Some don't even have an account pic. Some have one function. Some repeat the same words over and over again…. But this is mainly for small accounts. These have one function only, and it is "to make mass". Bigger, leading accounts will look more credible.
- *If the account is real, is it trustworthy?* There are famous accounts that spread fake news. If you are a social media user, you will know quite a few by now. If you are new, be very careful when you join them.
- *Does the text use the first-person pronoun?* Even when writing, we feel uneasy when "putting ourselves in the lie". So, many liars will avoid saying "I" and "me" and at times even "my" and "mine" ("my" is a possessive adjective, not a pronoun to be exact…) This will be more common with less experienced liars though. Very experienced ones may even suffer from the opposite. Why? They know that these pronouns inspire trust.
- *Do they repeat some key words?* By this we mean, are they just spreading a hashtag? Or a key word to pass on a message? Some even repeat the exact text as others, but when you see that someone is repeating a phrase over and over again, that account is trying to drill it into your brain… That is in itself a sign of dishonesty.

- *Are they specific or general?* Sometimes, the statements are so general that they will prove very little. But you will see the one that tells you about his cousin who... They have become smart, you see? They know that this will look trustworthy. Probe them then. Ask for more and more details until you find contradictions.

Then again, with the written word, the key strategies remain the old-fashioned ones:

- *Check the logic behind the text.* You need to find mistakes in the logical processes, contradictions, false reasoning etc.
- *Check with other sources.* Look at opposing views. They may enlighten you a lot!
- *Check the source or origin of what is being said.* Someone tells you that there is water on Mars? Check with a scientific source about it (by the way, there is and even on the Moon!)

Finally, use commonsense. No, it is very unlikely that a distant relative in a country none of your family has ever even mentioned has left you a fortune! Yet many people did fall for those emails...

Never trust people who make first contact and propose a deal or ask for money...

FROM LIES TO EXPRESSION

So, we looked at reasons why people lie, different types of lies and liars. But we also looked at how you can spot lying people and even which type of liar you are dealing with. And we also dipped our toes into a sister field, linguistics as applied to lying with written words.

Next, we will delve even deeper into the realm of body language... Ready to dive into what your body manifests?

12

SPEED-READING PEOPLE

Have you ever heard about speed-reading? I am talking about words here. If you read word by word, as many people do, your speed will be limited to about 140 words per minute. "Not bad," you might think – but wait till you hear how fast the fastest reader in the world can read... Howard "Speedy" Berg is in the *Guinness Book of Records* for reading (and understanding) ... 80 pages in one minute. That's about 25,000 words!

And the first concept of speed-reading is to read whole sentences in one go rather than individual words. The same applies to body language reading... If you read a sign at a time, you will be much slower than if you *look at clusters*. And I have given away a "trade secret" of body language speed reading.

The difference may not be as big as with words, but we'll never know... Guess why? Most body language speed readers work for the intelligence services...

WHY SPEED-READ PEOPLE?

The fact is that Police personnel, army personnel, secret agents and border agents are all trained to speed read body language, simply because they need it in their jobs... Now, imagine if you have to identify a possible terrorist or threat in the time you go through the customs at the airport... You don't have all that time you would at a conference, a board meeting or a political rally...

You really have minutes, actually seconds, sometimes on camera, to read body language. If you have seen how body language speed-reading has been used in emergency situations you would've been blown away.

There are two things that strike you:

1. With what speed and precision, they can pinpoint even a small tell-tale group of signs, out of what would appear to most like normal behavior.
2. The professional trust their colleagues and superiors give them. They don't ask why or what exactly. The reader points and they jump into action.

Of course, then they need to find out if it was actually true. A body language sign is not enough to incriminate anybody... But it gives you the idea that body language reading has developed with skills and "tricks" to the point that it is constantly and routinely used for security and safety reasons.

And speed-reading is a great advantage.

DEVELOPING YOUR SPEED-READING

Of course it will take time, but little by little, you too will develop your body language speed reading. Let's get straight into it actually...

Now you do know quite a lot about analyzing body language, you have a little "tool kit" you can use to read even quicker, but first of all remember:

- *Be ready to change your reading, your assessment, especially with speed reading.*
- *Keep in mind that speed-reading is more limited than a full analysis...*
- *...but it is useful in emergencies or when you have little time.*

Don't get me wrong now... I'm not asking you to go out and come back with generic "first impressions"... We know all the issues with them.

I am asking you to go out and come back with *clues, a lead, a possible reading angle...*

So, ready? Take a very short time... Go to a busy place (a park, road, a shopping mall). Look around randomly and only note down the body language that strikes you. Let your eyes choose why and what... Five minutes maximum!

Quick? Okay, now make a list of the body language you noticed.

Done? Now, not all of them, this is a "snapshot", but... for some of them, can you give a sketchy interpretation. *And sketch is exactly the word we are looking for.*

What's so special about sketching? It is fast, okay, it is not a finished work of art. But above all, it is open to corrections... You see, you can hardly correct an oil on canvas painting, but you can use your eraser with a pencil sketch...

So, for example... The woman who was swinging her arms visibly (I am guessing what you might have noted). What could it be? She had some happy news, maybe? She just left work and is going to meet someone she likes a lot? Or maybe she's a bit tipsy? That's the sort of sketch we are looking for.

Now I will ask you for a reverse exercise...

Go out, again, for five minutes and in a busy place... This time I'm asking you to find, as quickly as possible:

- A happy person
- A sad person
- A confident person
- A distracted person
- A tired person.

Choose some of your own if you want but give each spotting a super short time. As short as you can.

Now, go back home and tell me: what *cluster of body language signs* told you that the person, was happy? Sad? Etc.

Now you see, do this exercise over and over again and you will become *faster at spotting clusters of body language signs.*

Note that these *clusters are flexible.* Not everybody has the exact same body language... But after you do it a few times, you will start developing general (and flexible) clusters, or groups of signs that immediately tell you a lot about the person you are reading...

Training and exercising are the best ways to develop speed-reading – like all skills indeed! Quick, easy to do exercises like the ones I have just given you are ideal. In fact, the key is in the repetition. When you do one of these exercises first, you will develop some skills, even improve your speed a bit. The more you do it, the faster you will become.

But are there any tricks of the trade? Of course there are, and here they are for you!

5 TECHNIQUES TO SPEED-READ PEOPLE

You guessed it; these are all tricks that come from FBI agents and the like... Do keep in mind that speed may go to the detriment of accuracy in some cases. This is simply because you have a "snippet" to go on. It's like reading a whole book fast, with verbal speed-reading, and there you will get a very good understanding, or simply reading a page but fast.

So, you can use speed reading even if you are observing a five-hour long speech (poor you!) and in that case, you will get a very precise analysis. But if you speed-read a person for a minute, then you will get a partial picture anyway. Still, you will get more than if you used normal reading.

1. Look for clusters of signs

We have already said it, and luckily enough, this chapter comes after the one on micro-expressions. You see why this is handy? You have learned micro-expressions as clusters, groups of signs. If one is missing in a cluster, you still get the idea that the emotions expressed is that... You only need 3 out of 4 or 4 out of 5 to say, "This is the cluster of micro-expressions for happiness," right?

The same applies to subconscious reading. We don't need all the signs of sadness to understand that a child is unhappy. Sometimes, we can't even see them all from where we stand. But when you see large tearful eyes you will also expect all (or most) of the other micro-expressions, like eyebrows raised in the middle, pouting lower lip etc.…

You do have clusters already, and they are often centered on the emotion or state of mind they express together rather than a precise sign on its own. So, take the key archetypal emotions and states of mind and make a quick list of all the signs you know about them. Those will be clusters. These clusters can be very large, including 20 or 30 signs at times. But you will only need a handful to make a fast but accurate analysis.

So, complete the list as you wish, but don't forget happiness, sadness, anger, discomfort and frustration, negativity, positivity, aggression, honesty and openness, dishonesty, and a closed attitude.

Make a list for each then go out with one cluster in mind and spot the first person that displays enough signs for you to make a reliable assessment.

Do it again and again with all archetypes and you will see great results with your speed reading.

2. Know what you are looking for

Imagine you are an FBI agent and you are watching CCTV to spot a criminal walking in front of it after a crime. What would you look for? Maybe a hurried step, maybe someone who looks around a lot, maybe someone who is hiding his face, any signs of a fast heartbeat if you can etc.… You surely would not be looking for a skidding child, someone helping an old lady cross the street, someone walking with her or his heard in the clouds, would you?

The same as guided reading with words, fast reading is very focused from the start. Now, look for the word "sketching" in this Chapter. Found it? How long did it take you? Did you read all the words to find it? No, you exclude any word that does not look like it.

The same is when you are looking for specific traits. Try it out now... Go out and find everybody who is hiding his or her hands... Find all those who are focused on the destination of their journey, those who want to get somewhere. Then find those who are lost on the journey itself, like enjoying the view etc....

3. Do your research

If you know the person or sort of person we are talking about, start with possible scenarios. Going back to our intelligence agents, the more they know about the person they are looking for, the faster they can recognize them.

Anything can come in handy. Are they married? What sports do they play? Which TV programs do they like? In our case, however, as I don't think you are taking an entry interview for the CIA just yet, you may want to know some information about your clients, for example...

You see, if you know the client is a young and informal person, you may expect a very relaxed attitude and any signs out of it can be quite telling. On the contrary, if your client is an old and very formal person, any sign that shows lack of control may come from a strong internal negative reaction.

You see, you will be looking for very specific signs if you know your chickens. With friends, we can already expect a very clear set of signs, and we notice any small change...

4. Focus on discrepancies rather than individual signs

The previous tip leads us straight into the current one. The formal person having an informal sign. The informal one having a sign of stiffness. The manager showing a sign of fear. The speaker fidgeting. The bride looking at another man... Okay, the last was a joke but it gives you the idea.

Look for something that is not in line with what you would expect from that person, in that situation and at that stage.

5. Check what people are trying to hide

People use body language to project what they want you to see. So, make a clear distinction between:

- Voluntary body language
- Involuntary body language

Go out for your usual walk and find 5 clear signs of voluntary body language, and try to find 3 of involuntary body language... Again, repeat as necessary. Do it again and again until you feel that you are quick at dividing these.

Next, focus on involuntary body language. Sometimes, people don't mind about it. But if people are aware of it and try to hide it or control it, then you are on to something. That's a key indicator for those who are trained to spot the criminal, like border agents... The person who wants to *look calm but is not...*

MAKING FAST ASSESSMENTS OF BODY LANGUAGE: THE 5 C'S

There are two stages however with speed reading body language. One is being quick at spotting relevant signs and clusters of signs. The other is being quick with the conclusions, or better with the assessment.

Use these 5 C's to guide you in your analysis, and yes, we have seen them already (some in detail, one, "culture" will have its own chapter soon). But now is a good time to make a point and a summary of them all. And they all start with C.

1. **Context**, something we have talked about at length. Look for signs and clusters that look out of context...
2. **Clusters**, so... don't get side-tracked by the odd sign, focus on the groups of signs. Having said this, do keep the odd but unusual sign in mind... Come to it later and you may make great use of it... As you will find out from the bunch of flower story (I'm teasing you again!)
3. **Congruence**, which of course means that you need to look out for *congruence between what people say and what their body language says.*
4. **Consistency**, by which we mean that the person is consistent not just with the words, but with his or her personality, the situation etc. Try to get a baseline behavior you expect from a person and work from there. And this is why studying the person beforehand is very important.

5. *Culture.* Please take into consideration how culture affects body language... We have talked about it a lot in theoretical and general terms (nature vs. nurture again?!) and have seen some examples, but this is so important that we'll come back to it in a lot of detail.

All these, as you see, are practical and useful strategies and tips to speed-read people. But maybe nothing matches a particular quality you may have (or will develop!) *emotional intelligence.* And this is what we are going to see next!

13

ARE YOU EMOTIONALLY INTELLIGENT?

There are things no amount of mathematical computations can solve. Like, what do we feel looking at a child crying? It's like there are two worlds out there: one made of "things" that we can "count" and another world made of "feelings" which we can hardly describe...

Both are real (at least the emotional one is real, we are not sure about the physical one, but this is philosophy). But one is very much prompted by society (maybe because "things" can be sold for other "things" called money) and the other is at best underestimated, at worst repressed and criminalized.

I remember studying "the condition of women in Victorian Britain" at university and under the pretense that they were "innocent" and "angels of the hearth", there was a big prejudice: *women were seen as emotional and irrational.* That meant that women "were not fit to run the country, the economy" etc. – actually, not even fit to vote!

Yes, things have moved on, but what does society propose when we think about the word "intelligent"? A mathematician? A physicist? Whatever – we think about a *rational person.* Then I could keep complaining and say that actually the highest IQs are in categories where rationality is at least on a par with emotional intelligence... Writers for example... I could complain that Einstein, the world's "epitome of rationality" displayed clear signs of a very deep emotional intelligence and he did say that he used a lot of irrational thinking. In fact, like another giant of physics, Dr. Micho Kaku, Einstein spent most of his time meditating, like a Buddhist monk, not scribbling long formulas on a board, like they show us in *The Big Bang Theory*.

Do tell me to stop moaning – but not before I say the last thing... How many people are not regarded as intelligent only because they are not primarily rational? Sorry, mine was a crusade against injustice...

Nowadays, however, the importance of emotional intelligence is becoming clearer and clearer...

Even talking about body language, the emotional intelligence side of it is quite important. You see, we have broken down body language signs to the smallest bits, really... But there is always that "something" that does not add up rationally. And because I am stubborn, I am going to explain it to you.

Let's copy Einstein and make a thought experiment.

A means B, okay? So, a yawn means that you are tired or bored.

And this is correct, and we can read it rationally.

But if this is the case, why do people also understand body language signs they have *never seen?* Especially facial expressions are a wonder of this field and a great puzzle. There are some we can break down into clear signs, into "body language words" but there are so many facial expressions that it is as if you are "reading a new language" every new face you meet. And yet all studies show that we don't need to learn the new language to understand it, at least subconsciously.

That's because *even with body language we do not read and interpret everything rationally.*

So, the question now is...

WHAT DOES IT MEAN TO BE EMOTIONALLY INTELLIGENT?

Our mind works on different levels. Actually, the mind is not the brain, and the brain is not even all in our head. We have at least another brain in our heart (neurons) and one in our intestine (more neurons).

Then again, the brain does not follow a single method when understanding the world. You see, rationality and deduction are ways of thinking and understanding the world. So, if I say that A means 3 and B means 4, and I ask you, what is A+B then? You would use your rational mind to say, "A+B is 7!"

That is logic, that is rational thinking.

But when I ask you to explain what you feel when you hear Beethoven *Ode to Joy* you will not go down a logical process. You can't say the note D, followed by the note F etc. gives me happiness, uplifting feelings, ecstasy etc.

Yet you do have an answer, but to give it, you need to use your *emotional intelligence.*

There are many theories about why and how we use emotional intelligence... At a very visceral, if you want ancestral level, if you need to work out all the logical processes when you are running away from danger (say a lion)... the chances are that before you end solving the "equation" you have become a delicious meal for the lion.

Yes, because rational thinking may be exact, but very often it takes a lot of time.

We could even get to a long technical analysis of that beautiful piece of work that is *Ode to Joy,* but after years and years, we still would need to use emotional intelligence to say what we feel about it...

So, you are emotionally intelligent if you can "read feelings" and "think intuitively" (as opposed to deductively). But there is a bit more... You are emotionally intelligent if you can express yourself creatively.

So, to recap, emotional intelligence has three main elements:

- *Understanding feelings*
- *Using intuition*
- *Being creative.*

But note, *there are many levels of emotional intelligence.* Some people have impressive levels, we don't even realize it many times. I used to know a man, I am not joking, who would literally feel a sad person walk into a busy disco club. Impressive and I still regard him (he was a man, a gay man to be exact) as the person with the highest emotional intelligence I have ever met.

What is more, *you can improve and develop your emotional intelligence,* just like you can improve your memory and your rational intelligence.

Finally, though *the three elements are related, you do not need to have all three at the same level.* In my experience, it is hard to develop one to very high levels without having the other two at sound levels too...

Great artists can express themselves so well because they also understand feelings and they are intuitive, but maybe their intuition is less developed than their creativity... See what I mean?

Not everybody has good emotional intelligence, though. You may remember sociopaths and psychopaths. We met them when we talked about liars, big liars and manipulators in fact. These people, you may remember, have a very serious psychological condition, a pathological disease if you want: they do not understand that other people have feelings. They may "know" it, but they have no sense of *empathy.*

Right, in their case, their emotional intelligence is low or non-existent (there are, of course, different levels of sociopathy and psychopathy). So, one thing is sure... *Not having emotional intelligence or having a very low level is a serious pathology, a disease.* Actually, it is a disease that makes people dangerous for society.

9 SIGNS THAT YOU HAVE HIGH EMOTIONAL INTELLIGENCE

But how would you know if you have good, or even excellent emotional intelligence? We are about to find out. Again, take these signs as general guidelines, and each will have different levels, degrees, even development stages. And you do not need to have them all, nor all at the same level, to have good emotional intelligence.

One thing though: *people with good emotional intelligence are naturally good body language readers, and reading body language develops your emotional intelligence.* It's a virtuous cycle.

These are the 9 signs that tell you that you have good or even above average emotional intelligence.

1. You are easily moved

This is the most straightforward, telling and indisputable sign of emotional intelligence. Being "emotional" was once seen as an insult, as a flaw... and it still is for many people. However, if you watched *Schindler's List* and you were not moved, then your emotional intelligence needs improving. While your friend who starts sobbing even during a comedy – well, he or she has a very, very high level of emotional intelligence...

2. You identify easily and with people who are different from you

The ability to understand people who are not similar to us (in age, class, education, skin color, sexual orientation sex etc.) is a clear sign of emotional intelligence. Actually, when I say people, I mean also four-legged people, like dogs or cats... or six-legged people, like bees and ants...

Put quite simply, a very emotional intelligent person may even feel for the fly trapped on a windowpane. I know, many people would regard this as "silly". But that is a very emotionally intelligent person. At the same time, a person with low emotional intelligence may even find it hard to understand a puppy's eyes. Similarly, a person with low emotional intelligence may empathize only with similar people to him/her. An intelligent one will empathize with a wider range of people, if not all.

3. You are often unsure

Strange, isn't it? There's a myth that intelligent people always know everything... Not true. Even a rational person will need to doubt before s/he reaches a decision. Otherwise we would confuse arrogance and cockiness with intelligence. If to this, you add the fact that *you feel the impact of your opinions and choices on the world and others...* Then you will see why an emotionally intelligent person often has big moral dilemma and doubts.

If you are the one who sat at the back of the class waiting to give your answer, because you wanted to be 100% sure. If you did it even because you knew that a bad answer has emotional consequences (even for yourself), you likely have a high emotional intelligence. I would like to write a pedagogy book on how the school system actually represses emotional intelligent students, and you are having an insight right now...

4. You forgive and forget

It may sound counter-intuitive that sensitive people forget and forgive more, but all studies and statistics show they do. And by a measure. Psychopaths, on the other side of the scale, do not forgive. But that's because they see people as "objects to manipulate".

On the other hand, if you understand that you not forgiving someone makes that person suffer, you will try your best to put your feelings behind and make their life better.

5. You sometimes feel vulnerable and protect yourself

The relation between "feeling for others" and "feeling for yourself", the outside vs. inside world may well be one of the biggest leitmotifs of psychology as a whole. So, we can't go through it fully here.

But... it looks like feelings and emotions are what goes through this barrier quite freely... People who display a sense of care and love for others also often feel vulnerable themselves. People who don't care about other people's feelings also tend to underplay their own feelings. It's the macho thing, in simple words.

You can see yourself as a permeable membrane... You feel for others when they suffer but you are also easily permeated by feelings when others act in a way that affects you. Put simply, you feel sorry for people when something bad happens to them, but it also takes less for other people to make you feel bad.

Very sensitive people often (but not necessarily) show signs of shyness, embarrassment, and you will every now and then need that "time to yourself" or "away from all of it" ...

6. You are very susceptible to positive and negative

I know I am talking to an emotionally intelligent person because you thought, "But who isn't?" I read your mind again! (Only joking, of course!) The fact is that not everybody is severely affected by positivity and negativity. Some people are actually quite indifferent to it.

I'll reduce it to a very simple example... A beautiful color and an ugly one. People who are sensitive to the positivity or negativity of colors have high emotional intelligence. So, look around at what your office colleagues wear, and you'll find out that quite a few people are not *that* emotionally intelligent (it's a partial joke, but you get the point).

7. You have a complex relationship with criticism

This point is not as straightforward. What it means is that:

- *You give constructive criticism* (rather than using criticism for put downs). And this is easy to understand.
- *You can respond well to criticism.* But... you can also be offended by it. It all depends on whether it is *positive* and the way it is delivered. If someone criticizes you with malice, or with strong words, or in public, you may take badly to it.

8. You naturally mirror people's body language or language in general

We have talked about mirroring and we will get back to it in a few chapters. But it's like when someone sits one way, you too sit that way. When someone smiles, you smile back naturally. If someone speaks informally, you immediately switch into informal language...

These are all very strong signs of empathy and emotional intelligence. But this does not mean that you do it all the time... You will do it easily, but only with people you get on well with.

9. You have a good relationship with nature

Research shows that emotionally intelligent people appreciate nature at a very deep level. If you are one of those people who look at a sunset and you feel your heart swell... Then you are emotionally intelligent. If you feel at one with nature when you are in a park, you are emotionally intelligent...

Compare with people who only see nature as a resource... Do you worry if they cut down a forest to build factories or do you think, "Well, I can find another forest if I really need one for a picnic"?

I am sure that now you are starting to see why emotional intelligence is important to analyze body language but also how *it helps you project body language that makes you appear authentic and reliable.* "How," you may ask? Well, for this, you will have to wait a little bit... But not too long – promise!

14

NEGATIVE PEOPLE: PROTECTING YOURSELF AGAINST DARK INFLUENCE AND MANIPULATION

Because you're emotionally intelligent, you'll be very sensitive to people with negative influence on you. You know, the person you have a gut feeling about? That colleague "your skin" tells you is bad news? That neighbor you have the impression has ulterior motives? But how about those your emotional radar does not detect?

I am not trying to scare you. Not everybody is out to get you. But there are negative influences and even "dark", hidden influences in your life. If you don't find them out early, they may develop into "toxic relationships" (there are other factors too for such relationships...)

What is more, clearing your social world (professional and personal) of negative people and influences will make you a happier person, a more successful person and a person with fewer problems. Finally, if you want to become an influencer, or a person who wants to lead others, this is a necessary step to start this path or career.

In a board of directors (or any place where decisions are made and there are many people, like parliaments, school boards etc.) negative people will tend to lead to in-fights and repression outside. Now you understand why so many countries have bad politics...

If you want to set up, for example, a YouTube channel, you need to have honest collaborators, people who work for *your good*, not against it.

We will soon move into developing your body language professionally, to use it in your job and even become an influencer or a public speaker. But if you have negative people around you, even trying to manipulate you, no matter how much you work, things won't go as you would like them to. So, first of all... Let's see how people influence you negatively.

HOW DOES DARK INFLUENCE AND MANIPULATION WORK?

If you think that we are going into "conspiracy theory" when we talk about hidden influences and manipulation... Really, these have been used, studied and even taught (especially at university) for decades, actually, for sure for more than a century.

You may remember Ivan Pavlov, the man who did those famous experiments with the bell and the dog? The founder of that psychological school, known as *behaviorism?* Basically, you know that if you associate a sign with a positive stimulus, people sooner or later mix the two and at the sign they react as if they had the positive stimulus.

We're not that different from dogs! Pavlov's dog salivated when he heard the bell, because he associated it with food, even when there was no longer any food with it. People still smoke cigarettes many years after they realize that they don't look like James Dean... And why do vodka ads have to include some nudity? Nothing to do with Siberia, I guess... They associate two types of pleasures to do what? *To influence you into buying vodka.*

The whole of marketing can be interpreted as manipulation. So, you see, it has gone much further than we think. And there is a lot of body language in marketing... From the salesman shot from the waist up with a smile, facing the camera, wearing work or business clothes, a middle class haircut and the product in his hands (usually he was a man) to the celebrity witness, body language is used every day to tell you, "Buy this and buy that!" And most of us obediently comply...

If it works for television, it will work in face to face interaction – what do you reckon? And in fact, it does. Salespeople do it every day. If they were not good at that, they would not have a career... Politicians of course do it all the time too... But there may also be your "friend" and your "colleague" among them.

So, what are the key principles of manipulation?

We have already seen one:

1. Repetition

Why are ads repeated over and over again? They become even unbearable at times. But they don't care, do they? No, because the more you repeat a message, the more it sounds true. This is actually a manipulation of what we think is reality.

What's the best pasta brand? What's the best whiskey? The best milk? Water? Most of us will have a "clear" idea about these questions. But it's not even "their idea" and it is not "clear", rather it is "stubborn" ...

This happens also at a personal level. *People who manipulate you will repeat the same message over and over again.* And by "message" I don't only mean "verbal message". The Don Giovanni who steals hearts to "use women for a night" will do it with a very attractive body language, with many nonverbal signals with a clear message. One will not do the trick, and patience is, of course, one of their great qualities!

2. False personality

You see I remember everything? There was a very famous case among secret agents. The CIA was after a spy... But you know, double agents learn how to act, literally. They change the way they talk, walk, their body language and true, sometimes even use disguises... But this one was very good...

One day though, a CIA agent saw a little clip of him, and he was carrying a bunch of flowers... They arrested him, and on arrest, he said, "It was the flowers, wasn't it?" Do you know what happened? He bought a bunch of flowers and carried it with the flower heads down... Simple, we usually hold them up in the West... In fact, he was from Eastern Europe....

This is an extreme case, but it shows you how deceit and manipulation works. Good manipulators put on shows, create characters, and they make sure that they are credible. Don't get me wrong, these are skills one can learn consciously (like for double agents) or not... Some of them just find it natural to "change mask" ... In a way, we do it every day as well. You don't have the same personality with your partner and with your bank manager, do you? They see it as an extension of this normal behavior. But while we do it just for social norms and to a limited extent, they do it to manipulate and very often at very high levels.

3. Thomas's Theorem

This is a sociological theorem, and it is used by manipulators... The fact is that *a manipulator wants you to act upon a stimulus.* He or she wants *you* to buy that rusting car... They want *you* to help them with their career etc.... So, they need to *convince you to do something.*

And here Thomas's Theorem comes in handy. It says, "If men define situations as real, they are real in their consequences". Basically, you *only need to believe that something is real to react to it with real actions.* You only need to "think you need a new smartphone" to buy one. You don't actually have to need it for real...

You see this is at the core of advertisement but also of manipulation. So, *manipulators will convince you that you need to do something.*

They will need to *convince you of an untruth,* therefore. Or at least they would need to *overstate a problem to get the answer to it that they want from you.*

4. Reverse psychology

The idea of reverse psychology is to pretend to want something, knowing that the person who needs to act will do the opposite of what you want. So, if you convince them that you want the opposite of what you actually do, you end up getting the person to do what you wanted in the first place.

Yes, it sounds like one of those speeches Sir Nigel Hawthorne gave as Sir Humphrey Appleby in *Yes Minister* and *Yes Prime Minister.* In fact, the character is Machiavellian. And by Machiavellian, we mean people who will stop at nothing, including lying and cheating but, above all, manipulating others in order to achieve their goals.

5. Seeing people as "objects"

If you want to manipulate a person, you need to treat that person as an object, as "instrumental to your aims". Politicians treat whole sectors of society as such, very often. And here we come to some old "friends": sociopaths and psychopaths.

These people are manipulators like few others. In fact, very sadly, sociopaths and psychopaths often make amazing careers in business and politics. For them, you are like a washing machine, something to use till you are useful. Then throw away.

These people and manipulators do not see you for your intrinsic, emotional or social value... No, they see you as an "investment". Even when your friend, who actually does see you as a human being, uses you for something, at least in that situation, she or he has seen you as an object. And this is why we then "feel used".

6. They move you by degrees

Do you remember that famous evil manipulator, Iago, in Shakespeare's *Othello?* He's the primary example of how a manipulator works. And he follows all our steps. He pretends to be a friend of the Moor, he uses reverse psychology, he repeats his lies etc.... But he also moves Othello's mind step by step...

Manipulators move your position on a topic by dint of little, almost imperceptible shifts. This way, once you realize you have "moved to the dark side" it is too late, if you realize it at all. Many psychological and sociological studies about how Nazism came along show that people did not even realize that they were changing their position and embracing outright evil.

So, if you hate video games on a matter of principle and they want you to buy their own brand... Well, they will slowly move you into "not being that disgusted by video games", and "maybe not all are bad", and "some actually have some good features", then "even if I try one I will not like it," but "I will try one", to "it's not my cup of tea but it was better than I thought" and then with a few more steps you will wake up in the morning saying, "I can't do without you" as if you were a chain smoker...

7. Time!

As a consequence, manipulation takes some time in many cases. People who want to manipulate you, first of all will need easy access to you. Then they will need constant access, and time, of course.

DEVELOPING A DISCERNING EYE

Most of us have been fooled, conned, grifted and cheated upon in life. Now, you have seen how manipulators act. It's a very unpleasant topic, but you should look on the bright side, actually on the bright sides:

- You now know how they work.
- You know about body language, and this will help you spot them.
- You are going to learn how to keep them at a distance.

And there is more... Maybe your best tool to spot a manipulator is your emotional intelligence. You must have had that friend who "always knows from the start if a person is trustworthy or not"? Well, that friend, if s/he is right, has a very good emotional intelligence.

And of course, you need to look out for clues, and develop a discerning eye:

- *Look out for differences in the way the person behaves to you and others*. It is amazing how people sometimes are blind. They think the boss who butters them up but is horrible to others is doing it because the boss likes them? Keep dreaming.... They are just being used.
- *Look out for unnatural, contrived behavior.*
- *Look out for excessive kindness.* By this I mean excessive according to the person, your relationship with the person, the culture and of course, the situation. The man who screams about how great your average shoes are has something else in mind, most likely.
- *Look out for sudden changes of behavior (and body language) when*

he spots you. For example, if you walk into the room, or if s/he suddenly sees you etc.

- *Look out for insistent behavior.*

5 WAYS TO PROTECT YOURSELF

So, what can you actually do to protect yourself from toxic and manipulative people? Here are a few tips for you!

1. Control your emotional involvement

This is very difficult, especially in personal relationships. But even there, as soon as you start realizing that a "friend" is using you, *start a journey of emotional distancing.* Start coming to terms with the idea that you may not be friends much longer... Start going out with other friends. Start "filling in the emotional gap" that your breakup will cause.

For colleagues and people you work or deal with, this is easier. However, emotionally intelligent people will still suffer quite a lot. There are people who do not get emotionally involved with colleagues, for example. That may be necessary sometimes, especially if you work in a very unpleasant and competitive place. That's where manipulators concentrate.

2. Do not try to change them

In most cases, these people will not change for you. Do not get taken by the "good Samaritan" calling to save a person who is using you. To start with, the risk is that they will work out that you are trying to change them, and they will use it as an excuse to keep close to you and manipulate you even further.

Sociopaths and psychopaths especially will. And they will even think you stupid for wanting to help them...

3. Do not confront them face to face

That would be a waste of time in many cases. Furthermore, after denying the whole story, some may want to take revenge on you. Remember, not everybody has your moral compass, and if you have stumbled upon a dangerous person (again our antiheroes, psychopaths and sociopaths) the fact that you know about them will be seen as a threat by them! And they may want to render you harmless, maybe by discrediting you with others, lying about you etc.

4. Push them away slowly but steadily

Invent some excuses as to why you are not acting upon their trigger, so, why you are (no longer) falling for their trap... Then, little by little, cut off all meetings, all contact and all communication.

The more carefully you do this, the less s/he will realize what is happening and try to counter your move. Not only, but the less s/he will take offense, and as you know, these can be vicious people sometimes.

5. Go slow with relationships

There are friends you will trust with your life... How long have you known them for? A decade? Two? Five? The fact is that because we have good friends, we may be fooled into thinking that another person who, for some traits, reminds us of them is as trustworthy...

Instead, it may be a chance or, if you have met an experienced professional grifter, like those who marry rich partners to then steal their property, that person is actually imitating your friends' body language, personality, language, style etc. to gain your confidence.

Go slow and go safe. This is by far your best defense against manipulators.

KNOW WHO YOU ARE FACING AGAINST

Once you realize that there is something "fishy" about someone, start working out:

- Their real personality (key and hidden traits, like greed, envy, careerism)
- Their motives, their aims
- Their tactic and strategy.

Try also to assess *the gravity of the situation.* I mean, it can literally go from a dishonest shopkeeper to someone who wants to marry you to then bankrupt you... In your business life, it can go from a person who just wants a small advantage to the one who has decoded to end your career.

Beware, again, of sociopaths and psychopaths. Do throw in the "empathy test" like telling him or her that you are not comfortable with something. Do it even more than once... But if you get the idea that they don't feel anything. Steer away from them as fast as possible. And remember, they are not good at faking empathic feelings because they don't actually know what they are...

SPOTTING A PERSON WITH CONDESCENDING ATTITUDE

Very often, manipulators and toxic people are condescending towards their victims. I'm just watching an impressive six-part docu-film on Totò Riina, the most horrible mafia boss in history. I am amazed at how condescending he was, and he showed it, as a way of showing his power...

Here are some body language signs that the person has a condescending attitude you can group into a cluster to help you:

- *Chin upward and forehead moved backwards.* This is a very typical sign, so much so that it may even be voluntary.
- *Chin thrust.* This is when the person thrusts his or her chin forward. It is a sign of lack of respect for you, lack of consideration.
- *Sideway glance.* Looking at you from a three quarters position with the corner of their eyes, they are showing you that they do not trust you and they look down on you.
- *Literally looking down on you.* Lifting the head or moving it backwards to look down on you is another sign of condescension.
- *Nostril stretch and sneer.* Making a sneer with the mouth so that the nostrils are stretched out is a sign of disgust and condescension.

Sometimes, they may try to hide them, so, look for these with great care.

RECOGNIZE THE BODY LANGUAGE OF AGGRESSIVE BEHAVIOR

Things may get bad and out of hand, and you may end up being threatened, not only physically. Many bosses use threatening body language just as a way of establishing their power. Some politicians do too.

What is more, people who are trying to manipulate you or harm you may, every now and then, show signs of aggression which they do not notice or control. In the end, manipulation and aggression share many traits, and are even the same thing from some points of view. They are a way of using others, in both cases the victim is seen as inferior and even dehumanized etc.

So, here is what you need to look out for. Again, see them as a cluster.

- *Chest pushed outward towards you.* This, at all levels, is an aggressive sign.
- *Shoulders out.* Especially if visible, they may be a threatening position.
- *Belly out.* This too, unless the person has eaten far too many beans, may mean that the person has negative intentions or a negative attitude towards you.
- *Fists and stiff arms.* That's what boxers do before they start punching, so, not a nice sign from someone who is in front of you.
- *Mouth tips visibly turned down.* That is a sign of displeasure, but it can also show anger. in fact, ...
- *All signs of anger and condescension* we have already seen.

Phew! This was a hard chapter in many ways. I know and I understand you. It is never nice to talk about negative things, and especially people. But we had to do it and I thank you for getting through it.

As they say, "bad things happen" (okay, they use another word!) What we can do is be prepared for them and move on... and, talking about moving on... Next we will talk about how you can use body language to become the person you want to be... Something very positive indeed!

15

BECOME AN INFLUENCER

D o you want to run your own vlog or podcast? Or maybe you actually want (or need) to become a public speaker? Maybe you have a political career in mind? Or perhaps you are a teacher and you want to improve your presentation skills? And what's a manager giving a presentation in front of a board if not an influencer in suit and tie (metaphorically, especially if you are a woman...).

All these "activities" and "roles" rather than necessarily jobs, are *influencers.* You see, in life, even in most jobs, we switch from *influenced to influencer* regularly. A teacher is an influencer in class but not necessarily when talking to colleagues. This is why we should see it more like a role than a job.

Having said this, there are now famous professional influencers. Social media have made it possible for many people to launch their own channels, and they all need to use their body language correctly, even professionally, to become one.

HOW CONFIDENT ARE YOU?

Confidence comes back again and again in this book. We have seen how you can develop your confidence, and here we want to step back for a second and look at this topic again.

What we want to assess here is how "naturally" confident you are. Naturally is not really correct (nature vs. nurture again!) What we mean is *what is your baseline confidence level*, because more than natural reasons, what makes people confident or not are social and personal experiences (nurture). We do not have a "confidence gene" ...

This means a lot, as you may understand. But it does not mean that you can or cannot be an influencer. If for example your answer to this question is, "I am very, very confident," you may think that you can start working as an influencer straight away. But it may not be very wise! On the other hand, if your answer was, "I am not confident at all," you may even think you are not cut out for this role, while I would suggest that you start straight away!

No, you have not stepped into a parallel dimension! The fact is that people who are sure about their confidence may fall into three categories:

- Those who think they are more confident than what they really are.
- Those who are so confident that they appear arrogant.
- Those who actually are confident.

It is quite hard to assess one's own confidence. A dictator would say that he (most times, but theoretically she) is very confident. In reality most psychological analyses of dictators show that they have major psychological problems and they confuse arrogance with confidence (which often they lack!)

I am not saying that you could be a tyrant... But many bosses fall into this category. And they think they are confident, but to you, they appear as "bossy" or even "bullish".

The risk for people with this tendency, once they become influencers, is that their "cocky" and arrogant side comes out more visibly. How many famous people, especially journalists, commentators etc. start off as "confident and competent" and after a few years on TV they are outright arrogant and insufferable? I won't mention names because I don't fancy being sued, but I am sure you have plenty examples of this.

If you already are very confident, you need to avoid the "confidence back feed" you get from being an influencer. Do *you* remember Pavlov and the dog with the bell? Well, getting positive rewards and feedback for being an influencer can really affect your ego... you get used to it and then you take for granted that people owe it to you. Like the dog with the bell and food, you will expect the food (metaphorically) every time you hear the bell (post your vlog, make a speech etc.) ... And that very expectation of recognition is arrogance.

If you fall into the second category, you risk being very disappointed and even "wounded" if things go wrong. You need to understand that "losing face" in front of people is much harder than most people think. There are famous politicians who think they are confident just because they are on a winning streak, but as soon as they get criticized, they take it personally, badly, and even reject the criticism... That's no sign of confidence...

Keep in mind that if you have a vlog and something goes bad, you will have people annoying you for a long time, potentially forever. If you are an actor and you get heckled or booed in public, it will stick with you far longer than the end of the show. It will even be difficult to go back onto the stage. If your boss puts you down after a presentation with your colleagues, you will have to work with them after that.

And how about if you are not confident? That's a reason more to start practicing!

In all cases, what you need to do is *start small! Start on a small scale, with a small audience and build from there.* Whether you are confident or not, you will have a chance to correct yourself. *Keep modest if you are very confident and boost your confidence if you are not as you go along.*

What is more, *start with a friendly audience.* Even if you want to just run a vlog, start circulating it among friends, maybe, or on a small and friendly platform...

Finally, *take criticism constructively.* Your best friend is a *critical friend* who tells you honestly what you need to hear... People who surround themselves with yes-men sooner or later find at their own expenses that stroking their ego was not a replacement from doing a good job.

And what about your body language? *What is the "right" body language for an influencer?*

Hold on, we need a whole section on this...

THE CORRECT BODY LANGUAGE FOR AN INFLUENCER

You know the question. Now the answer: *it depends!* Disappointed? Maybe but you know we are going to find out... What does it depend on?

- *The topic*
- *The audience*
- *The format*
- *Your persona.*

You will want to look *confident, competent and in control all the time.* For all these variables... But in different ways.

Now, make a little film in your mind (a mind experiment like those Einstein used) ... Faduma wants to become a businesswoman and she decides to run an online vlog on "how to run a business". What will her body language look like? Jot down a few ideas (even mentally).

On the other hand, Sam too wants to run an online vlog, but the topic is hip hop music... Fine, now, what will Sam's body language look like?

You see, even with the same format, the different topic calls for different accents, levels of formality, typical gestures etc....

The audience is often strictly related to the topic. You may expect Faduma's audience to expect a more "canonical, institutional and contained, mainstream" type of body language than Sam's.

Similarly, nowadays there are many online influencers who specialize in wellbeing, spirituality and self-help. You will expect them to project calm, health, peace, serenity etc.... More akin to the Dalai Lama than a car salesman or a politician (don't correct me; I know the Dalai Lama is also a politician, but not your typical one...).

Here too, *try to put yourself in your audience's shoes...* What would you expect? What would you find "grating" and out of place? Try to match your viewer's expectations.

But this is not the whole story... Now, Faduma is making her vlog for university students and young entrepreneurs. That means that her body language can afford some informality and friendliness. But now, Faduma has been asked to present the exact same topic of one of her vlogs in front of a board of an important international corporation. Do you think she should change her body language?

I would think so. Most boards are run by older people to start with. They are also fully focused on the topic, and they don't need anything to keep them engaged. They also tend to be very formal, and in many cases, even very aware of their social position...

Once you have achieved the right formula with topic, audience and format, you can add some traits that set you apart from others, and make stand out, but without looking out of place.

You would look very silly if an estate agent opened a speech or video with the "Latin kings" sign (the horns with the fingers rappers do) ... That is extreme, but it shows the point...

On the other hand, to make sure you are recognizable, and you stand out, use:

- *Signature signs.* These are signs that people use to start or finish a speech or video etc. They are used by viewers to *identify the influencer or speaker.* Look at professional influencers and they all have one... it can be a wink, a sign with the hand, a small gesture... But it is always the same, accompanied by the same words (greetings) and moderate but clear.
- *Cultural signs.* These may refer to your culture, if you wish to project it, but also the culture related to your topic. For example, many healers and spiritual guides online use the "namaste" sign quite often (hands with palms together, like praying). That immediately tells the audience, "We have the same cultural background, we believe in the same things."

- *Personality signs*. These may be small personal identifiers that you scatter through your performance, rather than at the beginning or the end... Again, these should be moderate and in harmony with the topic and your personality.

INFLUENCER'S MOVEMENTS

Take a topic you are really passionate about. Get your smartphone out, and improvise a speech about it. Now watch it... I bet the first thing you notice is that you keep moving...

We move spontaneously when we speak, and the more we are engrossed in the subject, the more we move. Unfortunately, this works at times, but it will not work most times. The odd politician who shows great passion may stand something to gain. If it becomes a regular habit, that politician may end up looking deranged (like Hitler, Mussolini etc....).

This, to be honest, has its trends too. Recently, we have seen a trend in favor of politicians looking "engrossed" at the same time as we have seen a radicalization of politics. The two things go together, and politicians most often fake being engrossed in the topic when they shout and scream and beat their fist in the table... It's a show.

This is also very tiring for the audience and after a few years we go back to more "boring" body language from politicians, who nevertheless look more in control and tire the audience less. It is physically and emotionally demanding to watch an agitated person who keeps moving.

So, back to your video... One of the key things to learn especially when videoing (but also on stage) is to *keep still in front of the camera*. That does not mean completely still, or you would become boring. But:

- *Try not to move your chest.*
- *Try not to touch your face* (it's not a problem of looking dishonest, though some viewers may even see it as that, do it and watch it: it just is annoying).

- *Try not to move your head too much and especially not up and down.*
- *Focus movement in your eyes, hands and arms, and keep it slow and contained.*
- *Try not to move parts of your body (hands etc.) out of shot.*

As you can see, there are quite strict rules when you want to make a video and you also want to be taken as a professional influencer. Look at all the famous ones and check it out: they all follow these rules.

You will be relatively freer at a live event. But if you are being videoed, then again, you will have to *play to the camera and not to the live audience.*

CLOSE OR TOO CLOSE?

How close should you stand to the camera or your audience? It's an important point, very often neglected or underestimated... To start with, we need to understand the concept of *distance.*

Physical distance also indicates interpersonal and social distance.

You will see pop stars who get away with amazing close ups. But the relationship between a music star and their audience is incredibly intimate. They really have a love bond with their audience, who knows everything about them, feel they are friends and even family members. That's why it works for them. Similarly, your aunt or sister may send you a video with a "big face" and that would be okay.

Now, imagine being on a video conference with your boss and colleagues and they had the same "big face" as your sister's... No way! You would feel embarrassed, too intimate, uncomfortable.

So, we go back to our proximity zones, intimate, personal, social and public... *The distance from the viewer, spectator or camera will depend on the relationship you have with them.* In most cases, even with a camera (I am really thinking about your vlog), keep a *social distance.* That, as you know, is between 3 to 10 feet approximately.

In a monitor, you should aim that when you see your face, on a landscape image is between 2/3 and 1/3 of the height of the frame. Even there, look at the huge difference there is between a face that takes up 2/3 of this height (quite intimate, string eye contact, high emotional impact) and one that takes up only 1/3 (more impartial, respectful if you want, and detached).

This too will depend on what sort of podcast or speech you want to give. Even HM the Queen has different shots in her New Year Speech (to mention an old friend...) Very often, the camera starts from a distance and zooms in when there is an emotional touch. A closer face has a stronger emotional impact.

So, even Her Majesty's cameraman seems to follow our rule.

BODY LANGUAGE TIPS FOR INFLUENCERS

For an influencer, body language is an essential skill. Few people have actually made it in the public sphere without good body language abilities. Some, maybe extremely talented scientists or artists, buck the trend. But they are few and they do have exceptional skills in other areas. For most people, even with very good skills in their "trade", body language is a determining factor of success.

You are now learning how to use your body language skills. And we have seen some important principles. Now, it's time to "hone your skills" with some practical tips... Here they are!

1. Always get a "third person opinion"

You never actually fully appreciate how you "appear to others". Especially at first, get a friend to check on how you appear live, how your speech sounds and looks, or how your video impacts the viewer.

Actually, real professionals will do it even when they are at the top of their career, like singers take singing lessons even when they are at the top of the charts... If you know someone with some experience in "the trade", treasure their opinion. I am talking about actors, directors, drama teachers, public speakers, media experts, photographers, camera operators and the like.

2. Develop slowly

You will need to build your repertoire of body language slowly. But even once you are professional and established, *keep developing and improving your body language, but do it step by step and slowly.* A "sudden change of character" may strike your audience as odd, unfamiliar, even suspect... Don't risk it!

3. Learn from experts

Keep watching and observing other people in your field and influencers in general. *Read and analyze their body language.*

Experiment by mirroring and incorporating some of their body language into yours. Before you actually "make it public" and use it in a speech or vlog, please:

- Check with a friend if it works.
- Make sure it fits in with your persona, theme, topic, audience etc.
- Only use it once you feel you have "made it yours". It's like driving a car, you need to feel it is natural before you can drive one.

4. Be ready to change

Developing your body language does not just mean "adding signs"; it also means "eliminating signs". In the end, you never know how your audience is going to respond to signs... Even signs you think are great may end up being a total flop. Don't take it personally and get rid of them if necessary.

5. Never make the step longer than the leg

This is an Italian saying, which means that you can only bring changes that are well within your abilities... Remember when Theresa May, the former UK Prime Minister tried to look young and trendy, to give herself an image make up by dancing while walking on stage?

Why was it a disaster? Because she is not a very "smooth dancer"? Yes, that too. And a politician is not usually seen as the person you would dance with... So, she pushed it too far and did not have the skills to do it. Let's learn from other people's mistakes...

6. Use your mirror

We said that your mirror is your best friend. So, use it! Even if it will never give you the eyes of a viewer, even if it will never be the same as the camera, rehearsing in front of the mirror is excellent practice.

It will give you an immediate feedback loop from you do to what you see. This way, you can correct yourself immediately, without the risk of naturalizing, or internalizing a sign, a gesture, or a move, which would then make it difficult for you to correct it.

7. Strike a balance between rehearsal and spontaneity

However, sometimes we look at a speech, a video, a presentation and we say, "It does not sound real." On the surface, however, it looks "perfect". So, what is it that strikes as "perfect but not real"? It's the lack of spontaneity.

The sales agent that repeats the rigmarole to perfection, even with the right gestures, but fails to look like it's the first-time s/he has ever said this has few chances of getting your interest – let alone your money!

In a way, there is a big concept from the theatre we need to keep in mind here: *no matter how much you rehearse a play, you need to remember that each performance is a unique event in time!* It's not like re-playing a movie. It's a here and now event, with its own presence and you need to make your audience feel they are witnessing a unique event.

Don't worry if you will use it almost exactly the same tomorrow... as long as they "feel" you were not just repeating words...

And so, you see that body language is central to the role of influencers, but that what matters is that you build your own personal style, that fits your field, your medium and, of course, your audience.

But how about if your vlog or speech is meant to be seen in the UK rather than the USA? Or how about if you are doing a video for your Japanese customers? How would you need to change your body language?

16

CULTURAL DIFFERENCES IN BODY LANGUAGE

L et's take a coffee on a terrace in the Sorrento Gulf, near Naples, Italy... Wonderful scenery, amazing sea and impressive sunlight. The food is great, and the people gesticulate like they are putting on a show! Quick flight to London, not that far, and we go to a tearoom... There, you will see, the Sun – well, it's gone – the furniture is lovely, but people seem to be hiding all their gestures. Actually, the more you look like a marble statue, the more you fit in.

Yes, you guessed right! We are back to the nature vs. nurture leitmotif... Cultural differences (nurture) can really affect body language, to the point that you can recognize a person's nationality but not only (also class etc.) from the way s/he moves, gesticulates, stands, underlines what s/he says etc.

Keeping in mind your possible aspirations as an influencer, the *culture your audience mainly identifies with is also important to develop your body language.*

Similarly, if you ever happen to have a job where you need to deal with people from all over the world, you will need to be aware of gestures and body language that is (and, above all, is not) appropriate. This does not just include international negotiators and salespeople, even TEFL teachers will need that, or maybe if you decide to go traveling and you want to fit in...

IS IT APPROPRIATE?

We have seen that there are things that look "normal" in a county and may get you fired in another, for example putting your feet on the table (okay in the USA, not in other places). But there are also smaller signs that may not put your whole job at risk, but they may "give the wrong impression" especially subconsciously. And you know what that means...

To start with, let's state a general rule:

Less is more when it comes to body language and different cultures.

What do we mean by this? Especially if you are on a business trip (or similar) the idea is to "level your body language to a minimum" to avoid misunderstanding. Every unusual gesture would stick out like a sore thumb.

This, of course, does not mean that you should become a robot, that would make you appear boring, artificial and even give the impression that you are hiding something. However, try to reduce the size and frequency of your gestures.

Keep within your intimate zone

This is quite limited, but look for example at a Japanese businessperson... They will take up as little space as possible, keep their hands and arms to their sides as much as possible; they will sit upright and avoid stretching their legs out...

Asian people are very much aware of other people's spaces. This is due to a culture that values the "awareness of the other", and it does it much more than most western cultures. There is also an awareness that "space is shared". That's why they can live in small (but very tidy) spaces compared to Western people... But this also means that *taking up excessive space is regarded as utterly rude, inconsiderate and bad manners.*

If you are having a meeting with people from all over the world, *use the minimum denominator*: small gestures, little space taken etc. as a form of respect for everybody.

Looking at body language at these meetings will also show you how it is going once you get experienced with these things.

Be adaptable

Having said this, we need to look at the other side of the coin. *A stiff and very restrained body language can be taken as "untrustworthy" in some cultures, for example Mediterranean ones (including South America).*

Spanish, Italian, Portuguese cultures as well as many African cultures have a very expansive form of body language. Contact is common even with strangers, they easily go beyond the intimate zone, actually they tend to move almost freely into the social zone. Their gestures are more accentuated, and they welcome creative and unusual body language.

So, if you are dealing with people from these cultures, you may wish to be a bit more relaxed with your body language, however...

Do use mirroring but don't turn it into mocking

Mirroring, as you well know, is a key body language technique. But be careful... Use it in moderation and if you feel comfortable with it, or the result may be counterproductive.

Imagine if you kept bowing (as some Asian people do) at a meeting... On the one hand, it may be taken as a form of respect, on the other it may look like you are making fun of them. You see, you can *show respect for their culture, but you cannot appropriate it and you need to show respect for it with your body language. Remember that it is not your culture; it is theirs.*

Don't use signs and gestures you don't know the meaning of

They say that the Italian dictionary is in two volumes: one for words and a bigger one for gestures... It makes them very interesting for body language analysts, and you may feel very drawn to it. However, keep in mind that these many gestures have a very wide range of meaning, and some are downright rude and negative – actually, quite a lot of them.

Passing your fingers under your chin, stroking it with the tips of your fingers outwards, for example, looks innocent enough, does it? Unfortunately, it means "I don't care about what you are saying," and you can add an expletive after "care" to make the meaning properly correct...

Careful with feet

Feet are so important to body language, for many reasons:

- We are not very much aware of them.
- They have a strong connection with the ground, with the soil.
- They have strong cultural implications.
- They are often seen as unpleasant, and their use can be rude.

For example, in many Asian countries (Philippines, for example), showing the soles of your feet is at any time absolutely rude.

In some countries, however, like Arabic countries, people point with their feet, not their hands.

In some countries you need to take your shoes off indoors. This happens in most Asian countries but also Scandinavian ones. In other countries, like in Spain, taking off your shoes even indoors is rude... Keeping them on in Japan is rude...

So... Know what is expected of you. And the habit of taking shoes off indoors is spreading in many Western countries, but especially among "non-conventional" people, like liberal minded nature lovers etc.

Avoid touching people with your feet.

Avoid raising your feet above the knee. That is like a "borderline" of decency in many places.

In countries like India, feet are regarded as dirty, and touching the feet of the elders is a sign of respect, on the other hand.

In business situations, it is usually wise to avoid bringing attention to your feet.

On the other hand, a pop band will sit on the sofa with feet clearly in sight; that is informality, it makes them look at ease and "with friends" and it also draws attention to their sneakers, which, as you know are a cultural identifier.

There is a level of relativity in everything, including in body language and how you use it in different cultures.

What Do We Mean by "Culture"?

So far, we have mainly looked at cultures along one of its most common, easily understood and important determinants: origin, nationality, regional belonging... But culture moves along many lines:

- *Origin*
- *Age,* the cultural distance between generations reflects in body language too.
- *Education,* in fact, even within the same town the educational divide can be very marked.
- *Ethnicity,* which, in terms of body language, can mean different idioms altogether.
- *Cultural affiliation,* by which we mean every cultural variant, from

what type of music you like to your political, religious, spiritual and ideological inclination.

All these are factors that you need to take into consideration, in all circumstances, and, in particular, if you are trying to close an international business deal.

SUCCESSFUL INTERNATIONAL BUSINESS DEAL

International business deals, like deals between states, are a masterpiece of body language skills deployment. Look at the official photograph of an international deal between countries and you will realize how staged to the least detail they are. Where people stand or sit, who is on the right and who on the left, the handshake etc.… All is decided to give a precise signal.

On this point, for example, you will know that in the handshake, the man in the right always has the "upper hand" (yes, it's a pun) … They look more powerful because you can see the back of their hand in the photograph, while if you are on the left, your hand disappears behind the other person's, and you look less important… What is more, the person on the right shows the outside of her or his arm, the strong part, the one on the left shows the soft inside of his or her arm, the vulnerable part…

This is just to show you that it's a delicate business when we talk about international deals. Now, for example, at a business deal with Asian people, should you shake hands or bow?

This has changed over the years, as the position of Asia has changed. Especially when you are in Asia, nowadays the accepted protocol is to use both. Once upon a time, when the West was very dominant and the language of business was mainly US-UK centered, so was its body language. Nowadays, however, Asian economy is becoming more and more important and even business transactions are changing face, flavor, style…

US business style is fairly informal, and, in some cases, showing some arrogance is even encouraged. That is unacceptable in most countries all over the world and especially in Asia. It does not matter what kind of deal you are working on, if it is fair to both, if you are "shredding the competitor to bits" or on the losing side...

In international business deals there is *a very strong sense of formality. It's as if the behavioral rules were always the same. It's like a ceremony, with steps set out in advance that you will follow whatever the deal turns out to be...*

Hand shaking is usually ritualized; it will happen at the beginning, as a greeting, on agreeing the deal (that is actually a "let's shake hands on this") and it will also happen at the end, on parting, as a sign of friendship and a promise to keep the deal.

But this is not all... There is a very rigid sense of hierarchy and relative standing in these meetings. The most "powerful" person is the first to give the hand for shaking (in fact, with people like the Queen or the Pope, it is actually rude to initiate the handshake).

If you are meeting a senior businessperson and you give your hand first, you will look very ambitious, determined, and even careerist... To some people, this may even be a plus, but for most businesspeople that would usually strike as an affront, an insult to their senior position.

Similarly, seating is also very formalized; always wait for the host to indicate that you can sit down, and always try to sit down after the more senior people are present.

If there are Asians, do keep in mind that *seniority is extremely important for Asian people, and this includes age seniority.* Sitting down before a person who is older than you is a huge challenge to their seniority, while you are expected to bow first and lower. That can make the whole difference between a successful deal and a total disaster.

Sex can be a major issue in international deals... *In many countries, women are yet not considered equals to men.* This means that for women it is much harder to find a place around important international business tables and that even if they do, they will have stronger opposition, problems with prejudice etc. Their body language is very often scrutinized, so they need to be very good and careful indeed.

Apart from the general rules and setting of international business deals there are many things you need to be very aware of.

To start with *never show any signs of being nervous, restless or bored.* There is no tapping your foot, clicking your pen and fidgeting with your papers if you want to strike a good deal...

The "watching the time" gesture is really dangerous too. It is a sign that you want to get out of there, or that you are in a hurry. True, it is allowed, but only if done by the "chair", or the person who needs to call the meeting to a close. If anyone else does it, it may really give the wrong signals...

You also have to *avoid any signs of aggression or arrogance.* Leave Hollywood movies with cocky businessmen or women on the DVD shelf... They don't represent reality. Dealing with other businesspeople means trying to get the best out of them. They have something to offer to you, otherwise you would not be there. So, *respect is the key word.*

Nodding is generally seen as an agreement sign. You will have seen foreign secretaries and even presidents nod when a foreign politician was talking – in their own language... Of course, they didn't understand a word of what was being said... still, their nodding was taken the way it was meant to: as a general sign of agreement, more like a bonding sign than a commentary on the point.

So, do nod regularly, even if you don't understand what they are saying. But regularly does not mean all the time, or you will end up making a fool of yourself. *Try to understand when the person is making a point and nod.* Again, keep everything underplayed: a small nod, just a hint at a nod, not like at a heavy metal concert!

Finally, and above all, *never shy away from eye contact.* In fact, try to keep your eyes up, avoiding looking down (apart from checking on your notes). Let your eyes move around the room or place but keep them at the other people's eye level (roughly). Looking down can be taken as a sign of defeat, or a sign that you are in trouble. Looking up may give the impression you want to get out of there. Looking back, too, is a sign that you expect something different or something to happen or that you are seeking help.

Try to be ready to engage in eye contact and absolutely try to disengage at the same time as the other person. Interrupting it too early is a sign of lack of confidence and even dishonesty, staring at a person's eyes after s/he has moved away can be a challenge, appear insistent and even aggressive.

So, working on an international business deal is a matter of fine and delicate balance. You will really need to use all your body language skills to walk away successful. And now, to be honest, you are quite an expert of body language. But the good learner is the one who knows how to better himself or herself, and that's why the last chapter of this book is meant to help you become an independent and always improving body language reader and user...

17

APPLYING WHAT YOU LEARN

Look back at the journey we have made together... You have learned so much! From the basic principles of body language to shaping and developing your own body language, even at professional level...

But as you know, we never stop learning. In truth, people who become passionate about a topic keep studying it, updating their knowledge and becoming more and more professional well after their formal studies are over. And, who knows, new things may come to light even in our field...

So, this is not the end of your journey. But my duty is to make sure that you keep learning, that you keep developing your skills and that, from now on, you can do it independently.

The key principle of personal and professional growth is that you apply your skills, and even experiment them, in different areas of your life:

- *Everyday life*
- *Relationships*
- *Public speaking*
- *Work*
- *Negotiations.*

So, off we go!

EVERYDAY LIFE

You will have noticed that all our exercises only take up a few minutes and you can do them even when you are shopping, during normal everyday activities. There is a reason for this. Actually, there are many... To start with, we are all busy, and few of us have whole hours to dedicate to our self-development. Next, it is easier to learn something by small but regular efforts. Small mistakes also have more manageable consequences. Finally, it is by getting confident with the subject that you learn it best, so, by using it in your everyday life.

Keep using your body language reading skills on the bus, when you go shopping, when you are at work etc.... That practice is so essential to your development that it's like breathing or drinking water for us.

Find readings on the topic. It is fairly popular, which means that you can find articles online etc. However, in many cases these are not professional articles. A quick online search has brought up more urban myths than truths. But... There are professionals (and I will give you a reading list). To start with, doubt anyone who tells you "this sign always means this" ... Follow the core principles in this book and you will find it easy to tell a charlatan from a professional body language reader.

Make sure you use reliable magazines but above all, *watch body language readers in action.* These are always very insightful and great source of knowledge and information.

Set aside a few minutes every day to study and improve your body language. And give yourself breaks. Maybe five days out of seven, or even three would be fine. When? Find one of those blind spots we all have in our lives, those useless times like going to work, time spent in the bathroom, waiting for the bus etc....

Keep in mind that your body language must primarily suit you. Don't give in to pleasing others too much. Strike a balance; by all means try to improve yourself for your family and friends, but don't assume that you should do it uncritically.

RELATIONSHIPS

Reading body language can help you make wide choices when it comes to social relationships. Developing your own body language can help you improve your social relationships.

However, keep in mind the key principle: *a hurried assessment is most likely a wrong assessment.* Which is our old "don't jump to conclusions."

At the same time, *try not to use your friends and family as Guinea pigs.* Reading a bit here and there is fine, but always keep in mind that their value is as people, that they are important parts of your life and that you should never objectify them.

Prefer people you don't know well to read their body language. To start with, you will start with a clearer, less prejudiced mind. Secondly, you will not risk changing or even ruining important relationships. On the whole *avoid body language analysis with significant others.* This is not a "you mustn't"; it is, as it says, an "avoid".

If you do *use body language reading with significant others, then tell them that you have and what you have found out.* Body language readers sometimes use their skills in disagreements; well, after doing it, they should table a chat on equal terms about it.

In terms of improving your body language, social relationships can be a light on the one hand, or a cause of chaos on the other... Put simply, *you cannot change your body language to suit each and any social relationship individually.* You may have a repertoire that allows you some change, but you cannot tailor it to each individual.

You *need to keep a steady baseline with everybody.* If you change too much, people will notice it and you will appear fake, deceitful and untrustworthy...

Also remember that if you *experiment your body language with relationships, do it in small doses and small steps.* Do not face a friend with a huge change all of a sudden, or s/he can be disoriented, and your relationship may suffer.

PUBLIC SPEAKING

Public speaking is an art... I am thinking, some comedians are great in a play or TV series, but then you go to watch their standup comedy performance and it's a disappointment. This means that even trained professionals find standing in front of an audience on their own and speaking quite tough...

On this, a very quick tip: *timing is of the essence.* I can often see comedians deliver great jokes but then there's a split-second mismatch with the punch line and it does not work (or not as well). So, this means that public speaking is hard, but that you need to *keep working on your timing.*

Do not try out something that does not suit you in public speaking. It would be like the Pope telling a dirty joke. No matter how good it can be, it will never work.

Here, hitting *the right balance between being serious and cracking the odd joke* can make the difference between a good speech and a disaster. US Presidents on average have done that well. UK Prime ministers have traditionally failed.

In many business speeches, it has now become almost a format to start with a joke. Most *Ted Talks* start with a joke. And on average they are good ones... But make sure you *rehearse your intro joke to perfection and that it is a good joke!* Also, make sure it is a joke everybody can understand, but at the same time one that sounds original and not desperate.

Do not laugh during your joke but *freeze your face at the end.* That's the trick, you see... That is the nonverbal clue that the joke is over, and you are expecting the audience's response. Choose that freeze frame very carefully.

Of course, *watch as many public speeches as you can.* In fact, Ted Talks are excellent practice; you have a range of different speakers, topics and styles. Not all are super professional and not all are as successful. But that is an advantage, because you can see where you may go wrong, which is more difficult if you only watch great professionals. Add political rallies, business presentations and, of course, standup comedy!

Keep in mind that the audience is always different. Some audiences are very hard indeed. Don't panic, and *don't exaggerate your body language if the audience is hard and hostile.* That is a gut reaction but also a mistake. If they are hostile, they will read your exaggerations as buffoonery, and most likely they will not appreciate them.

WORK

Most of us spend the vast majority of our waking lives at work or in work related activities. This means that the body language we use at work can make a huge difference to our quality of life and even improve (or damage) out career chances...

So, some final tips on how to go about it...

First of all, *focus on your stamina.* You know that old employee who comes in every day at the same time and leaves every day after a hard day and yet it seems that he has made no effort? You know the young employee who comes in, runs around all day and goes home looking like a wreck?

Okay, the first has built physical stamina (PS: all studies show that old employees are more productive and there is a difference between activity and efficiency!). But if s/he gives you the idea that s/he can go through the fay with little or no effort it is because... Look at his or her shoulders! They stay up all day! So...

Improve your body language when leaving work. Do you think your boss does not see you leaving the office? Do you think that s/he does not notice that you feel the weight of the day on you? Now, do you think that, with a promotion to offer, your boss will choose someone who appears to sail through their days or someone who is already in difficulty at 5 PM every day? And your boss does not need to be a body language reader: remember that most of these ideas are formed subconsciously.

Control your body language as you progress in your career. If you have ever been to a canteen or staff room and heard the comments on people who have got a promotion you will know... Most of the comments, if negative, focus on the person's change of "attitude" (and body language).

Do not show your "former peers" that you feel superior. Good managers in fact will establish egalitarian relationships with the people they manage. That little lack of respect of appearing superior not only will cost you friends, efficiency and production. It may come back to bite you later on, when you are more vulnerable.

Pick times in the day to correct your body language. You see, you may start the day with a perfect posture, but as time goes by, you start slouching, bending over your desk etc.... So, I would suggest you focus on your body language when leaving home, when entering the workplace, at every coffee break, when you go to the toilet, every time you enter your boss's office and when you leave.

Pull the string. A simple trick that opera singers use is to imagine they have a string that falls to the ground from the very top of their skull, in the middle of the crown. You pull that string and align your body to it, and that gives you a perfect and upright posture. Like a puppet...

NEGOTIATIONS

Negotiations can be part of your work, but also of your daily life. Every time you go to a store or market you negotiate (maybe not on the price, but on the choice of items etc....) And we need to negotiate even in our social lives... You want to go to the cinema but your partner wants to stay home? Well, you'll have to negotiate it!

Negotiating is another difficult set of skills, maybe even an art (metaphorically). For this reason, body language is key to success. And here are some tips to help you develop it.

Use some regular negotiators. Try to have deals with the same people now you know how to read body language. This will allow you to see patterns of behavior and even small signs. You see, if you change partner every time, you only have a chance to see major signs. But if you want to hone your skills, you will need to analyze the same person many times.

Only experiment when the post at stake is low. If you are haggling over the price of a kilo of potatoes, do play with different body language signs etc. But if you are negotiating to get the job of your dreams, better safe than sorry.

Play games where negotiations are core. That will give you a chance to improve your body language when negotiating in a safe but educational way. Some card games have a lot of negotiating (and body language) in them. Monopoly and similar games too have the same elements etc.

Study great negotiators. There are now some TV programs that show negotiations but be careful. These are often faked and distorted. They have the "Hollywood narrative" of the tough and arrogant world. It is tough, and it is arrogant – don't get me wrong. But you don't want to be arrogant to someone who can give you a deal or give it to someone else...

That arrogance that exists (unfortunately) between boss and employee becomes kindness and even false servility when it comes to getting a deal you need.

Study different cultures. For example, Arabs are wonderful negotiators. On the other hand, they train for it... You go to a megastore and the price is fixed. Even at the grocer's the price is fixed. Well, in the Arab world the center is the market, where everybody haggles over the price all the time. It's expected; it's normal. So, even a child doing his or her mother's chores starts learning how to negotiate...

FUTURE DEVELOPMENT

Body language is a now a fully-grown discipline, which means that it will keep growing, but maybe at a smaller rate and with lesser "big discoveries" than in the past. When disciplines become "adult", they tend to specialize rather than go through revolutions.

But new things will come along, and you will need to know them. And, while we are at it, maybe you can keep a good diary of how your body language progresses, both in terms of reading and of your own development...

CONCLUSION

It looks like yesterday when we started this journey together. Personally, I feel it has been a very rich one, with so much to talk about, so many twists and turns along the road. For you, I hope it has been an enjoyable one and, above all, a useful and informative one.

Looking back, we have gone from the very principles of body language, how it came about and how it developed at the beginning to very advanced uses of it, including how to use it professionally…

Along the way, we kept swinging like a pendulum between reading body language and applying it to our own personality, how we present ourselves. A bit like reading and writing when it comes to verbal language: one is the "passive skill" and the other is the "active skill" as teachers and educationalists call them.

We have explored all the different fields of body language: kinesics, proxemics, oculesics etc. we looked at each part of the body in detail, from head to toe, literally, and many times… We also now know that reading what people communicate through their body is not a matter of "adding up discrete signs"; it's a holistic activity. You need to read individual signs within the general perspective, the overall appearance, a bit like reading words within a paragraph…

We have also applied our knowledge to many different areas of life: from private life to business, via social relationships, you now have a good toolkit to read what people actually mean with their body. What is more, you now have a wide and growing repertoire of body language signs and "idioms" to use for yourself.

Along this journey, as you well know, two words have cropped up regularly, "nature" and "nurture". This is not strange though... It has been a big dichotomy (or two ways of reading and interpreting reality) in philosophy and science since the times of the ancient Greeks.

And when it comes to nurture, we have seen how different cultures greatly influence how we express ourselves with our bodies. And with a world that becomes metaphorically smaller by the day, understanding these cultural differences may well make the difference between a bright and successful international career or ending up in a provincial office with no prospects of a better future.

And in fact, I hope you have appreciated the balance of theory and practice I tried to strike within this book. I apologize if I had to introduce (at times even advanced and complex) theories. On the other hand, thinking about it, I hope you have enjoyed it, because it is the theory that gives us those broad lines, we use to make sense of the world around us.

The many real, practical and I hope at times colorful examples of this book, however, may well be what will stick to your mind best. They are the "coloring" of this book. And we have had a few chances to smile and even giggle along the way.

And the exercises I proposed, I trust, were all easy to do and never took up longer than they had to. As we are about to part ways, maybe till our next book, do keep in mind that your improvement as a reader and as a user of body language will come from many, frequent and regular sessions and exercises, not from big chunks of time every now and then. It is a bit like learning a new language or mathematics: ten minutes every day are better than two hours once a week. And I wish I'd followed my maths teacher's advice on this when I was at school, maybe I'd be a famous physicist now!

It's also been nice to "fly" all over the world and see how different cultures use body language in different ways... We have traveled east and west, always with respect, and we have seen how even greetings change all over the world. And, along the way, we discovered that our feet, those often-forgotten parts of our body, can make a huge difference if we want to integrate in a foreign country, find friends from that country or strike a deal with people from abroad...

And we have also met people from all paths of life, from poor people and the way rappers use their hands to Her Majesty the Queen and the way she uses body language to project her authority... Because body language is also a manifestation of class, social values and even musical taste!

All has been "spiced up" with a lot of psychology and sociology, as these are the founding sciences behind body language analysis. And the parallels with linguistics, another science that informs our field, have been many and revealing indeed... But because our life is a kaleidoscope of experience, along the line we also ventured into art, music (classical and pop), literature and, why not, quite a bit of philosophy... All within the perspective of that "mother of humanities" which is history...

And if at the beginning of the book you were wondering whether body language analysis was a "quackery" or a real science, I trust you are now sure that it is a fully valid and "adult" scientific study. However, like with most fields, be aware that there are urban myths and misconceptions about it, especially online.

And we finally came to the point where you have to fly the nest... Maybe, and I hope so, we will meet again on the pages of another book... But if we do not, I wish you all the best in your personal, social and professional life. Now that you have made it to the end of this book, however, I can leave you with a calmer heart, because if you have made it this far, you *really* have learned a lot, and you *really have all the tools and skills to read body language correctly and in depth, and to use it to make your life a happier, richer and more successful one – on all fronts!*

RESOURCES

And if you want to explore this fascinating topic even further, here are some great reads for you to check out!

Cooper, B. (2019). *Body Language Mastery: 4 Books in 1: The Ultimate Psychology Guide to Analyzing, Reading and Influencing People Using Body Language, Emotional Intelligence, Psychological Persuasion and Manipulation*. Independently published.

Cooper, D. (2020). *Decode People Personalities: How to Analyze People by Knowing Body Language Signals & Behavioral Psychology. Understand What Every Person is Saying Using Emotional Intelligence and NLP*. Independently published.

Edwards, V. V. (2018). *Captivate: The Science of Succeeding with People* (Reprint ed.). Portfolio.

Goleman, A. (2020). *Manipulation, Body Language, Dark Psychology: How to Analyze and Influence People, Read Body Language, Avoid Deceptions, Brainwashing and Mind Control. Discover 9 Secrets to Stop Being Manipulated*. Diamond Mind Ltd.

Houston, P., Floyd, M., Carnicero, S., & Tennant, D. (2013). *Spy the Lie: Former CIA Officers Teach You How to Detect Deception* (Reprint ed.). St. Martin's Griffin.

Lowen, A. (2012). *The Language of the Body.* The Alexander Lowen Foundation.

McGray, P. P. (2020b). *Dark Psychology and Manipulation: How to Leverage the Secrets of Mind Control, NLP, Brainwashing, Hypnosis, Body Language in Dating, Relationships, and at Work.* Independently published.

McGray, P. P. (2020b). *Dark Psychology and Manipulation: How to Leverage the Secrets of Mind Control, NLP, Brainwashing, Hypnosis, Body Language in Dating, Relationships, and at Work.* Independently published.

Navarro, J. (2018). *The Dictionary of Body Language: A Field Guide to Human Behavior.* William Morrow Paperbacks.

Navarro, J., & Karlins, M. (2008). *What Every Body Is Saying: An Ex-FBI Agent's Guide to Speed-Reading People* (Illustrated ed.). William Morrow Paperbacks.

Rouse, S. (2021). *Understanding Body Language: How to Decode Nonverbal Communication in Life, Love, and Work.* Rockridge Press.

Segal, I. (2010). *The Secret Language of Your Body: The Essential Guide to Health and Wellness* (Reprint ed.). Beyond Words.

Williams, J. W. (2020). *How to Read People Like a Book: A Guide to Speed-Reading People, Understand Body Language and Emotions, Decode Intentions, and Connect Effortlessly (Communication Skills Training).* Independently published.

www.ingramcontent.com/pod-product-compliance
Lightning Source LLC
Chambersburg PA
CBHW030245030426
42336CB00009B/264